KU-515-942

CHANGED INTO HIS LIKENESS

Rhoda George

CHANGED
INTO
HIS
LIKENESS

WATCHMAN NEE

PUBLICATIONS

Fort Washington, PA 19034

Changed into His Likeness
Published by CLC Publications

U.S.A.
P.O. Box 1449, Fort Washington, PA 19034

UNITED KINGDOM
CLC International (UK)
51 The Dean. Alresford, Hampshire, SO24 9BJ

ISBN (paperback): 978-0-87508-859-4
ISBN (e-book): 978-1-61958-024-4

Copyright © by Angus I. Kinnear

First published in 1967

Unless otherwise indicated, Scripture quotations
are from the *New King James Version,* Copyright
1979, 1980, 1982 by Thomas Nelson, Inc.

This edition published in 2007
by CLC Publications,
Fort Washington, Pennsylvania,
by permission of Kingsway Publications, Ltd.,
Eastbourne, Sussex, England

ALL RIGHTS RESERVED

This printing 2014

Printed in the United States of America

Contents

Preface 7

1. Three Significant Men 9

Abraham: The Divine Choice

2. The Starting Point of Recovery 23
3. Call and Response 31
4. The Committed Life 43
5. The Man in the Land 53
6. The Heir and the Proof of Time 63
7. The Covenant of Grace 71
8. The Gifts, or the Giver? 79

Isaac: The Son Given

9. The Wealth of the Child of God 89
10. The Status of an Heir 97
11. The New Life Indwelling 107

Jacob: The Real Transformation

12. Precious Stones 115
13. His Own Medicine 123
14. The Divine Wounding 133
15. The Face of God 143
16. The Peaceable Fruit 151

Preface

THIS BOOK originated in a series of addresses given by Nee To-sheng of Foochow in the early months of 1940 to Chinese Christians meeting at Hardoon Road, Shanghai. I am greatly indebted to a friend whose notes, taken down in English at the time, have made it possible to reproduce his talks in the present form with no more than essential literary tidying-up.

The author starts with a practical exposition of the patriarchal story, designed to offer by analogy a solution of our own problems of Christian faith and walk by pointing again to the sufficiency of God in Christ in the face of human failure. Some readers may feel that they have heard much of this before, and be tempted to exclaim, Yes, but does it honestly work out in practice? It is a joy therefore to move into his important final chapters, where, with telling flashes of insight, he educes from the same exposition an impressive example of the real and radical transformation God in fact brings about in the man or woman truly committed to Him.

These chapters are, I believe, a valuable contribution to the understanding of God's ways with all His own.

Angus I. Kinnear
London 1967

1

Three Significant Men

WHEN in the Old Testament God sets out to secure a people wholly delivered from bondage and separated to Himself in a unique way, and when in order to do so He appears first to Moses at the burning bush, it is remarkable that He identifies Himself by a threefold designation. "I am the God of your father—the God of Abraham, the God of Isaac, and the God of Jacob" (Exodus 3:6). And when a little later God sends Moses to the Israelites to announce His intention to them, the same threefold expression comes as a kind of refrain through His pronouncement. "Thus you shall say to the children of Israel: 'The LORD God of your fathers, the God of Abraham, the God of Isaac, and the God of Jacob, has sent me to you. This is My name forever, and this is My memorial to all generations.' Go and gather the elders of Israel together, and say to them, 'The LORD God of your fathers, the God of Abraham, of Isaac, and of Jacob, appeared to me'" (verses 15–16).

Now we would surely not be wrong in asking ourselves, Why this triple refrain? Especially so since the Lord Jesus Himself uses the same expression in a passage which occurs in each of the first three Gospels. "But concerning the resurrection of the dead, have you not read what was spoken to you by God, saying, 'I am the God of Abraham, the God of Isaac, and the God of Jacob'? God is not the God of the dead, but of the living" (Matthew 22:31–32). Why is it, we would like to know, that God employs this threefold expression when He identifies Himself to mankind? What is the significance for us, His children, of these three recurring names?

The apostle Paul assures us that what is contained in Scripture was written for our learning, and here is something which is brought to our attention in both the Old and New Testaments. This suggests that in both the old dispensation and the new God is following one identical principle. In the old God appeared to Moses with the intention of calling Israel out of Egypt to become His chosen people. In the new Jesus appeared in resurrection to the nucleus of a new people of His choice. If now it is true that we who have been saved by His grace are of that people, may we not confidently expect therefore that with us He is following the same principle?

Again, what does God mean when He speaks today of "Israel"? Is there a larger meaning in the term than appears on the surface? For the answer let us look at the end of Paul's letter to the Galatians, where he writes of the new creation in which there is neither Jew nor Greek (6:15), but where all find their common ground in the Cross of Christ. Desiring peace and mercy for all who are Christ's, Paul uses of them the remarkable expression "the Israel of God." I tell you, we who believe in the Lord Jesus *are* the Israel of God, one with all the true Israel, not a separate people.

But further, if God has chosen us to be His own, then we are right to ask ourselves what history we must pass through under His hand to constitute us such a people of God. Surely it is as we study the lives and experiences of these three significant men that the answer to that question will be given to us. For Abraham, Isaac, and Jacob hold a special status in the providence of God and one not held by any others. Theirs is the privilege of leading us all to God in a unique way.

Let us go back to the beginning. As we know all too well, Adam yielded to the temptation to doubt God's love, and so fell from his high destiny and came under condemnation and death. In the course which he had taken, all his generations followed him—except Noah. Noah, the exception, was a righteous man and blameless. Noah found grace in the eyes of the Lord.

Yet Noah was one and alone; and we are given no clue as to how God dealt with him to bring him to the place where he "walked with God." He was righteous, but we are not told whether God specially chose him, nor how He handled him in order to make him righteous. In this particular matter, therefore, Noah has nothing to teach us, though of course there are many other lessons for us in his story.

But it is when we come to Abraham that we encounter the first example of a man chosen by God. Abraham was an idolater—but God chose him. "Your fathers, including Terah, the father of Abraham and the father of Nahor, dwelt on the other side of the River in old times; and they served other gods. Then I took your father Abraham from the other side of the River, led him throughout all the land of Canaan, and multiplied his descendants" (Joshua 24:2–3). Yes, God chose this idol-worshiper, laid hold of him, and said, "He is mine." According to His will He chose him. Today all God's people are like that. They have responded to His love, they have tasted His salvation, and now they find themselves His chosen. God possesses a people whose starting point is His choice of them.

Of course Abraham was not yet a nation, nor was Isaac. Nor indeed was Jacob, until he became Israel. But when Israel was called out of Egypt, then at last God had a people for His own possession. Thus God's people may be said to have had two beginnings: Abraham the man, and Israel the nation. First came the individual men of faith. When these had opened the way, then there followed the kingdom of Israel in its fullness. God's dealings with Abraham and with his son and grandson made possible all that came after. So the nation, we may say, is founded upon these pioneers. Without them there would be no Israel. Ultimately it is the combined experience of these three that accounts for the course followed by God's people on earth.

Do you wonder at the special position given to Abraham, Isaac, and Jacob? Surely it has something to do with the fact that God's name, God's character, is bound up with them. He *is* their God. When speaking to man, God so identifies Himself again and again. We have seen, too, that Jesus names them as evidence of the resurrection. Furthermore in Luke 13:28 He says, "You shall see Abraham and Isaac and Jacob and all the prophets in the kingdom of God." Once again it is just these three who are singled out by name. Everything turns on them. Why do they have this position?

Historically they had it because, as we have said, God wanted a people. Today they have it because God's present aim is precisely that—to take out from among the nations a people *for His name* (Acts 15:14). And that people's history begins with Abraham because God begins with Abraham. God worked in that man's life because he was to have a special experience to transmit to them, and of course the same is true also of Isaac and of Jacob. With each man God moved to the same goal, namely, to mediate to His people through him a unique experience of Himself.

Moreover, while it is a fact that God began the creation of a people with Abraham, yet He did not of course possess that people until Jacob's history was completed and the twelve tribes were in view. What the three of them went through therefore must *together* be the spiritual experience of all God's chosen. The history of just one or two out of the three is not enough. Nothing one-sided will meet the divine requirements. We should not content ourselves with a merely partial enjoyment. As the Israel of God we must have, in however small a measure, the full experience of them all. It is the intention of God that all His true people should say of themselves, "He is *to me* the God of Abraham, and of Isaac, and of Jacob." Let us not stop short of this. No doubt Ishmael could call Him "the God of Abraham," but that will not do. Esau could go further and say "the God of Abraham and of Isaac," but that too is insufficient. Spiritual experience is not summed up in Abraham and Isaac. Jacob's name must be included as well. To the true Israel He is the God of all their fathers.

Many of God's children say, "I have a lack; I am conscious of a need; yet I am unable to define what it is I need."

At some point in our history many of us seek from God a "second blessing," often with little clear idea of what the content of such a blessing may be. Let me tell you that it includes not one thing merely but three. In the pages that follow we shall seek to set forth from the history of these three patriarchs what is the nature of the threefold blessing God has for His people.

God is the true originator, from whom all His new creation springs. We might fittingly borrow here the words of the Lord Jesus, who said, "My Father has been working until now, and I have been working." This is a lesson we all have to learn; that we can originate nothing. God alone is the one who begins everything (Genesis 1:1; 1 Peter 1:3–5). Though this touches our pride, yet the day we really see this as a fact is a day of happiness for us. It means that, where eternal values are concerned, we have recognized that all is from God.

Abraham was not a bit like Noah. Noah, it seems, stood out as righteous in clear distinction from all around him. Abraham on the other hand was just like his neighbors, an idolater. Amid such circumstances God chose him. Abraham had no beginning of his own. God took the initiative. Nothing is more precious than the sovereignty of God. Abraham never thought of Canaan as his goal. He went out, not knowing whither he was bound, but in response to a call of God.

Blessed is the man who doesn't know! This man even moved "not knowing where he was going." When we really understand that God is the originator of all that matters in life, we no longer have such cocksureness about what we are going to do. We gladly say, "If the Lord wills."

Even Abraham's son came from God; he had to be given

in a unique way. Nothing that originated from Abraham himself, including his other son Ishmael, could serve God's purpose. He learned that God was the Father, the Source, the Fount of everything. Without Him there is nothing at all. Unless God does a thing, we can do nothing. Learning this lesson, we begin to be "the people of God."

Isaac is preeminently the son. He illustrates in a remarkable way the work of God in Christ. This is made very clear for us by the apostle Paul in Galatians, where Isaac, the heir, is said to have been born "according to the Spirit," and where we who are Christ's are called "Abraham's seed, and heirs according to the promise" (4:29; 3:29). "When the fullness of the time had come, God sent forth His Son, born of a woman, born under the law, that He might redeem those who were under the law, that we might receive the adoption as sons. And because you are sons, God has sent forth the spirit of His Son into your hearts, crying out, 'Abba, Father!'" (4:4–6).

Abraham is distinguished by what he did, by the great movements which started with him. Jacob is notable for the much suffering he passed through. Between these two great men stands Isaac, a very ordinary man, with nothing special about him except his ordinariness. As you read the Genesis narrative you cannot find any great feature by which Isaac is distinguished. Look at the following facts. Abraham, we are told, amassed much wealth; not so Isaac, Isaac only received the inheritance; he did nothing for it, nothing to bring it into being. What in fact did he do? We are told that he dug certain wells, but when we look at the story in Genesis 26 it appears at once that he only unstopped those which his father had previously dug and which had been filled up with earth.

What, then, is the lesson which Isaac teaches us? It is this, that we have nothing which we were not given. If nothing was by my own originating, then equally surely nothing is by my own attaining. As Paul puts it: "What do you have that you did not receive?" Abraham's experience is very precious to us, teaching us that God is our Father, the source to us of everything. But Abraham's experience without Isaac's is not enough. God is also the Son, the given One. We all know that forgiveness of sins is a gift that must be received. So also is victory over sin. We have nothing of ourselves that is not fundamentally God's gift to us. So we find that to Isaac God promised precisely what He had already given to Abraham (Genesis 26:3–5).

Isaac was born to wealth. We do not progress, we do not advance into wealth: we are born into it. This is true of every spiritual experience we have as Christians. For example, "The law of the spirit of life" which "made me free from the law of sin and of death," is something which I possess *in Christ Jesus*, not in myself. It is not mine as something I have attained; it is what I have received. It is like the miracle of life which keeps the birds in the air in defiance of gravity. It is designed to deliver us from sin and death; and it is God's gift to us. But how many of us Christians really know its secret? No wonder the sparrows think we have no heavenly Father as they have! Yet to be wealthy when you have been born into wealth is surely no problem.

We have said that the principle of Isaac's life is the principle of receiving. This can be seen in the difference between the wives of these three men. Except that she was Abraham's half-sister, we do not know who Sarah was nor where she came from. We know only that he brought her out of Ur of the

Chaldees with him. Jacob was a man who bargained for everything; he even bargained for his wife. He made his own choice. Isaac never even saw Rebekah before she was chosen. His father said who she must be, chose her, sent for her, paid for her dowry. In his role as son, Isaac received everything. And we, before God, possess nothing that is not His endowment.

So we come to Jacob. He presents us with another significant principle in God's dealings with His children. Many of us can see that God is the source of everything. We accept in theory at least that we have to receive everything from Him. Why then is it that so many of us do not take the gift, but go on struggling for it? The answer is that the Jacob principle, the principle of natural strength, so dominates us. We are so sure that we shall achieve God's end by our efforts.

This is why no teaching on victory over sin, no doctrine of sanctification is complete which does not deal radically with the strength of our nature. Without this essential the results they produce are transient only.

We who are Christ's are heirs according to promise, but the inheritance we receive in the Son, and the road which God wants us to walk in enjoyment of that inheritance—these depend upon the touch of God on our natural strength. Jacob was a most clever, able man. There was nothing he could not do. He cheated his own brother, deceived his father and contrived to relieve his uncle of all his possessions. But this cleverness, this talent for self-advancement had no place in the will and plan of God for him. It must all be brought to nought, and the experiences of Jacob by which this was accomplished well illustrate the disciplinary work of the Holy Spirit.

Everything Jacob set his hand to went wrong, even from

his birth. When the twins were born, we are told that Jacob's hand was found to be holding his brother's heel; nevertheless he was not born the elder son. He sought by guile to secure the birthright, but it was he who in fact had to leave home and flee. He had set his heart on Rachel as a bride, but he found himself first of all married to Leah. He set out eventually from Padan Aram with much wealth, most of it gained by questionable means, but he had to be prepared to give it all away to his brother Esau on the journey home in order to save his own life. Here is the discipline of the Spirit. God's hand is in judgment upon everything Jacob does while relying upon his own craftiness. People who are specially clever have to learn, if necessary through suffering, that it is not by the wisdom of men that we live but by God.

Jacob learned one great lesson. He was on the eve of losing everything, all he had accumulated, all he had worked for. He could think of a way of meeting man, and he devised a plan that he hoped would appease Esau and at least save his own skin. But then he met God. He met God, and was lamed. God had touched Jacob *himself.* Up to that day he had been Jacob, "the supplanter." From that day on he was Israel, "a prince with God." This was the beginning of the kingdom. We are not overstating the facts when we say that he was a different man from that day forward. He who had deceived others was himself now deceived by others, even by his own sons. The old, crafty Jacob would easily have seen through their deception. The new Jacob was completely taken in. He believed them, and wept, saying: "It is my son's tunic. A wild beast has devoured him. Without doubt Joseph is torn to pieces."

This, the breaking of the strength of nature, is the point to which all God's people must come. "Jacob was left alone; and a Man wrestled with him until the breaking of day." We may get along well enough in the dark, but the light of God is our undoing. We are finished. This is the discipline of the Spirit.

Abraham saw God as Father. He proved Him to be the source of all things. Isaac received the inheritance as a son. It is a blessed thing to have a gift bestowed upon us by God. Yet even what we receive we may seize upon and spoil. Jacob attempted to do this, and was only saved from the consequences by having his natural strength undone. There must be a day in our experience when this happens. The characteristic of those who truly know God is that they have no faith in their own competence, no reliance upon themselves. When Jacob learned this lesson, then in truth there began to be an Israel of God.

Let me say something to reassure you. God is not expecting to find those who are naturally "born good," and who therefore have no need for His dealings with them. He knows well that they are not to be found. He chooses ordinary folk like you and me, who are willing to receive from Him His gift of grace, and who are willing also to submit to this discipline in order that the gift should not be abused. Abraham displays the *purpose* of God in His choice of us sinners. Isaac shows us the *life* of God made available to us in the gift of His Son. Jacob sets forth the *ways* of God in the Holy Spirit's handling of us to conserve and expand what we have received. He cuts short our old, self-willed nature, to make way for our new nature in Christ to work in willing cooperation with God. Thus the Spirit moves to attain God's ends by His own means. This is the goal of all God's dealings with His own.

Abraham:

The Divine Choice

2

The Starting Point
of Recovery

WE BEGIN with Abraham because the divine plan of redemption begins with Abraham. When we open our New Testament the first words we read are these: "The book of the geneology of Jesus Christ, the Son of David, the Son of Abraham." Immediately the genealogy begins: "Abraham begot Isaac, Isaac begot Jacob, and Jacob begot Judah and his brothers." There can be no doubt, then, about Abraham's importance. Moreover, of all the Old Testament characters his is the name most frequently on the lips of the Lord Jesus. "Before Abraham was, I AM," Jesus says. "Your father Abraham rejoiced to see My day, and he saw it and was glad" (John 8:56, 58).

Everything began with Abraham; he is the starting point of everything in redemption and in the purpose of God. The apostle Paul tells us that Abraham is "the father of all those who believe" (Romans 4:11). Not Adam but Abraham; for Adam is the starting point only of human sin. From his day onward sin reigned.

Among the men who succeeded Adam there were, of course, those who shone as lights in the increasing darkness of those days. Abel was good; he offered sacrifices according to God's will, but he offered for himself alone. He was not specially chosen or prepared in relation to the purpose of God. Enoch, too, was simply an individual in his walk with God, and Noah was the same. None of these three was specially chosen by God in relation to the recovery of what was lost by Adam.

Abel, Enoch, Noah: all three worshiped God. Abraham did not; he worshiped idols. Things had gone from bad to worse, until the men in Ur of the Chaldees and in all the other cities around them were idolaters. And Abraham and Nahor and their father Terah were no different: "they served other gods" (Joshua 24:2). By himself Abraham was not morally the equal of any of those three men who went before him, Noah, Enoch, or Abel. By nature he was on the same level as Adam after his fall, or as Cain. Yet he was the starting point for divine recovery.

Through none of those who preceded Abraham did God set Himself to deal with the situation created by sin. Abraham was the first through whom He did this.

Between Adam and Abraham, God worked with men as individuals. In Abraham God went further, and began to deal with the question of racial sin. God's whole movement to undo the consequences of the Fall began with him.

Redemption is completed and perfected in Christ, but redemption began with Abraham. Christ is the center and the heart of God's redemptive purpose. Christ is the midpoint of the line of recovery, of which the kingdom of God in fullness is the end and Abraham is the starting point. For Abraham was not called and chosen for his own sake but for the sake of his descendants. He was called to be God's vessel in dealing with a tragic situation, not to receive something just for himself. To receive grace, and to transmit grace, are two different things.

When man fell, God took no immediate action. In Noah's day He judged the world, but He made no move yet to redeem it. Not until Abraham did He begin to deal with the situation at its heart. Abraham was called so that through him God might deal with the whole terrible problem of sin.

Right at the outset of God's call to Abraham we can see His aim clearly stated. "Now the LORD had said to Abram, 'Get out of your country, from your family and from your father's house, to a land that I will show you. I will make you a great nation; I will bless you and make your name great; and you shall be a blessing. I will bless those who bless you, and will I curse him who curses you; and in you all the families of the earth shall be blessed'" (Genesis 12:1–3). Abraham was called to an inheritance, and this is a question of land. He was called also to be a great nation, and this is a question of people. Through him all the nations were to be blessed, and this surely indicates the moral sphere of his call.

All God's work for His people is connected with a land. If they were faithful, they possessed it; if not, they lost it. From that land all enemies would be cast out, and they were to occupy it for God. "The land" is the central thought of the Old Testament. God wants a land for His own. It is not a question of the earth. In the Fall God lost the earth. Nor is it a question of heaven. Of course, there was never a problem about heaven. One day it will certainly be a question of recovery of the earth. God wants the whole earth back, and that will be accomplished in the fullness of His kingdom. Before that day, however, God wants a land. He wants that upon which He can take His stand as His very own. The land is His. It is at least one place where God can reveal Himself, can be heard and seen and can give to men His laws. First He has the land, then He will have the earth.

Today God still has "a land" in the earth, although it is not in one whole piece. In the past it was the territory and the whole kingdom of Israel. Now it is the Church, wherever the Church is in local expression—in Antioch, in Thessalonica, in Ephesus. It is still "the land," because the Body of Christ stands there. God's work of recovery begins with the land. Therefore every believer can stand for God and for His will in the place where he lives and works. He can occupy that piece of territory and hold it for God.

The recovery of the whole earth is based on the recovery of those portions now. As long as the people of God were in the land, God was "the Possessor of heaven and earth." When they lost the land, He was called "the God of heaven" only. When Melchizedek met Abraham after the battle of the kings, Abraham was already in the land. He could therefore say to the king of Sodom, "I have raised my hand to the LORD, God Most High, Possessor of heaven and earth" (Genesis 14:22). But the time came when Israel lost the land, and then Nehemiah writes, "I was fasting and praying before the God of heaven" (Nehemiah 1:4). Because they have let the land go, therefore the earth is lost to God.

Thus the land is not an end in itself; it stands for the

whole earth. God is thinking ultimately in large terms. "Blessed are the meek," says Jesus, "for they shall inherit the earth." This earth of ours, which will come back to God in fullness at the end of this age, is being won back now by the meek. Just as in the Old Testament the land of Israel was a sort of token of God's claim upon the whole earth, so the different portions where His children stand for Him now are a token of His sovereign right to the whole earth today. God wants us not only to preach the gospel and to edify and build up His Church, He wants us especially to stand on this earth for Him.

The New Testament parallel to "the land" is the expression we find in the Gospels: "the kingdom [or rule] of heaven." The land was the sphere upon this earth in which God's word ruled, the place where His power was effective. When the New Testament speaks of the kingdom of heaven it has in view just such a sphere in the earth today where the rule of God is effective. The question today is, does heaven reign already in the Church? It certainly does not anywhere else.

I think we will agree that this is more than an individual matter. It calls for God's children in a given place to stand together subject to His rule, so that through them His rule becomes an effective thing there. It is not only a question of the preaching of the gospel but also of the presence of the kingdom. The gospel of grace is for the salvation of sinners. The gospel of the kingdom is intended to bring back to God the earth which is His by right. Unless our work affects the earth in this way, it is falling short of God's purpose.

God used much time to establish Abraham in the land of promise. As soon as Abraham left it a little way, to go to

Egypt or to go to Gerar, he was in moral defeat. We spiritualize these things and draw from them lessons about Abraham's personal walk with God, but in doing this we may overlook something important. It is this, that God wanted the land because God wants the earth.

Then secondly, Abraham's call was not only a question of a land but also of a people. "I will make you a great nation." That was God's motive in calling this man to Himself from among a world of idolaters.

Conditions had greatly changed since Adam's day. Adam was judged and punished, and, as we have said, he was not thereafter concerned with the earth as a whole. The only demand made upon his generation was for individual godliness. They either sought after God or they did not. With the generation of Noah, however, something different is introduced, namely, a law (Genesis 9:3–6). Men were given the opportunity of cooperating together under a law of God or, of course, they could choose to do so apart from Him. From that time man became part of an organization. Babel is the great result of mankind's organizing itself, and from this ultimately comes Babylon, the counterfeit of the Body of Christ. Then, at the beginning of the world as *we* now know it, God chose out Abraham with a view to securing for Himself a people.

In Adam's time, and in Noah's, God dealt with the whole world. All humanity left Eden in Adam. In the Flood the whole world came under judgment. These were the disastrous results of the Fall. Now we come to the time of Abraham and God is going to begin a work that will undo the effects of that Fall. How will He do this? He is not going to sweep the whole world back to Himself willy-nilly. He will work to secure a people through whom He can win the world. Abraham is the beginning of the choice of God, and he was called not only to lay claim for Him to a land but also to secure for Him a people.

The greater part of the Old Testament is taken up with the record of God's people on the earth. Have we realized what it means to say that God has a people on earth? Suppose we belong to a business house having widespread overseas interests. How confidently we say, "We have a man in Tokyo, or in Manila," meaning a representative in that place. That is just what God has in His people on the earth, and that is how He would speak of them. As soon as Israel turned from God to idols they lost their position as the people of God—and God lost His people. "The land has committed great harlotry by departing from the LORD. . . . Call his name Lo-Ammi, for you are not My people, and I will not be your God" (Hosea 1:2, 9). They might commit other sins, and then they were a sinning people but still the people of God. When, however, they fell into idolatry they were no longer His people. He had to repudiate them.

The nation of Israel was to be a witness to God, a people who enshrined God's presence. Where Israel was, Jehovah was. When their foes came against them it was God they encountered. To deal with them they must deal with God. While Israel was true to God it held a unique position, apart from and superior to the other nations. That was gone as soon as they yielded to idolatry. Where God has a people now, He has a witness; where He has no people, He has no witness.

The call of Abraham has a special character, unique in the Old Testament. There was nothing quite like it, for this was God's first great reaction to the Fall. It was the beginning of His answer to the problem of sin. Abraham was to reveal God as the Redeemer who calls men out of a world of idolatry to faith in Himself.

What is the Church today? She is the people of God, or in the words of Acts 15:14, "a people for His name." As God once committed His purpose to Abraham so today He has committed everything to His Church.

It is not enough therefore just to preach the gospel for individual salvation. That must be done, and every one of us must seek to win men individually out of the world to faith in Jesus Christ; but let us understand the motive behind such work. It is not just that the sinner should be saved and should arrive at a place of security and contentment. God wants a people for Himself, who will confess Him before men. Every born-again child of God must be taught to take his place in that witnessing people. For God does not deal directly with the nations today, but through the Church which is His Body. It is to take our share in the task that we have been called, and God desires that we should find our place there.

3

Call and Response

THE DIVINE activities in this age can be shown to have two great aspects, the direct work of God according to His eternal purpose, and His remedial work of redemption. In the revelation of Scripture these two interlock. We may distinguish between them but we cannot separate them. God's work of recovery contains both a remedy for sin and a reaffirmation of His eternal purpose for man.

Even when God is dealing with the first step, justification, He has the goal always in view. That is why we are told in Galatians 3:8 that the Scripture, "foreseeing that God would justify the Gentiles by faith, preached the gospel beforehand to Abraham, saying, 'In you all the nations shall be blessed.'"

Abraham was the first man to receive the call of God. He was called because he was chosen; the call implies the choice. And he was chosen for no other reason than that God was pleased to choose him.

In the book of Genesis, God makes three beginnings: with Adam at his creation, with Noah after the Flood, and with Abraham at the time of his call. Noah was sent forth into the new world which he was appointed to govern. His generation saw the beginning of organized social life, of law between man and man. God's legislation through Noah was designed to give that new world a moral character, from which, however, it turned away.

Abraham's task was a different one. He was not called either to administer or to legislate for the nations of this world; indeed, he was to turn his back on the world. He already had a country of his own, but it was his only to leave. He had a family—to leave. He had a home—to leave. He looked for the city which has foundations (Hebrews 11:10); he himself had no city. He was a pilgrim. Unlike Noah, he was to establish and to improve nothing. Noah had a task to do: to establish order and to give divine instruction to the world. Abraham in his life gave nothing to the world. He was a pilgrim, called to pass through it. His links were essentially with heaven.

Abraham was called out of the world. "By faith Abraham obeyed when he was called to go out to the place which he would receive as an inheritance. And he went out, not knowing where he was going" (Hebrews 11:8). There is no call except to come out. Abraham was at home in the world with its established order, its advanced culture, its justifiable pride of attainment, and he was called to come out of that world to fulfill the purpose of God. That is the divine calling. There had been nothing wrong with Noah's way of dealing directly with the world in order to improve it; it had been God's appointed way for Noah. But when it led nowhere, and when accordingly God set Himself to His long-term task of recovery, He began with the call to Abraham, not now to improve the world but to come out of it.

Today God's principle of working is that of Abraham, not of Noah. At Ur of the Chaldees it was not that God had forgotten the world but that He was going to deal with it through Abraham, and no longer directly. Through this one man He would deal with the whole world. Abraham was the vessel into which God's wisdom and power and grace were now deposited, in order that through him God might open the door of blessing to all men.

How then, we may ask ourselves, should one chosen as God's vessel for so great a task know his God? For the responsibility resting upon this one man was tremendous. To use man's finite way of speaking, the whole plan of God, the whole divine will and purpose for man, depended on Abraham. It stood or fell with him. Need we wonder, then, that Abraham had to go through so much trial and testing in order to bring him to know God, so that men could speak of "the God of Abraham," and so that God could call Himself by that name without moral violation?

Abraham, we saw, is the father of all those who believe. This is an interesting expression, for it shows us that all spiritual principle is based on birth, not on preaching. Men are not changed by listening to some doctrine or by following a course of instructive teaching. They are changed by birth. First God chose one man who believed, and from him were born the many. When you meet a man who believes and who is saved, you become aware that he has something you do not have. That something is not just information; it is life. He has been born again. God has planted living seed in the soil of his heart. Have we this living seed in us? If we have, then we must give birth to others. Paul spoke of his "sons" in the faith. He was their spiritual father, not merely their preacher or counselor.

The nations are blessed through Abraham, not because they hear a new doctrine but because they have received a new life. The New Jerusalem will witness the perfection of that blessing of the nations. It was Abraham's privilege to begin it.

Abraham's story falls naturally into two parts: his call (Genesis 11–14) in which the land is the central theme; and his posterity (Genesis 15–24) in which, of course, Isaac figures predominantly. We begin with the first of these.

We shall best understand the call of Abraham if we see it in its proper setting. "The God of glory appeared to our father Abraham when he was in Mesopotamia, before he dwelt in Haran" (Acts 7:2). Nimrod, the mighty rebel, had established his kingdom in Babel. His subjects had set up their great tower in the land of Shinar, and they had been scattered. The nations everywhere had not only forgotten God but, as we have seen, were idolaters. The whole world worshiped false gods, and Abraham's family was no exception. In this Abraham was very different from Abel and Enoch and Noah. They seem to have been men of backbone, strikingly different from all those around them. They stood out against the stream and refused to be dragged along by it. Not so Abraham. He was indistinguishable from those around him. Were they idolaters? So was he. Why, after all, should he be any different?

The work of God started with such a man. Clearly, then, it was not in him, in his upright character or in his moral determination that lay the source of his choice, but in God. Of His own will God chose him. Abraham learned the meaning of the fatherhood of God. This was a vital lesson. If Abraham had not been just the same as all the rest, then after his call he could have looked back and based his new circumstances on some fundamental difference in himself. But he was not different. The difference lay in *God*, not in Abraham.

Learn to recognize God's sovereignty. Learn to rejoice in God's pleasure. This was Abraham's first lesson, namely that God, not himself, was the Source. Our salvation is entirely from God; there is no reason in us at all why He should save us. And if this is true of our salvation it is true of all that follows from it. If the source of our life is in God, so also is everything else. Nothing starts from us.

From Acts chapter 7 we learn that Abraham was called by God while he was yet in Ur of the Chaldees, before he came to Haran. In his first words before the Jews' council Stephen begins from this fact. "Brethren and fathers, listen. The God of glory appeared to our father Abraham. . . . Then he came . . . and dwelt in Haran." That was enough. The man who sees that "glory" knows he must respond. He cannot do otherwise. Stephen himself was in a tight corner when he said these words; but at the end of his terrible experience we are told (verse 55) that being full of the Holy Spirit he gazed into heaven and saw the glory of God, and Jesus standing at the right hand of God. He who appeared to Abraham at the beginning and He whom Stephen saw at the end were one and the same God of glory. In the final issue, what is an extra stone or two to one who sees the glory of God?

Both the call of Abraham and the reason for his response

lay in God. Once behold the God of glory and you must believe, you cannot do otherwise. Thus it was by faith—faith in the God of glory—that Abraham, when he was called, obeyed to go out.

But, you say, my faith is too small. I could never have faith like Abraham's!

This is where Genesis chapter 11 comes to our help. If it were not for Stephen's words in Acts we would never know that God had called Abraham while he was still in Ur of the Chaldees. If we had only the account given to us in Genesis we would get a different impression. In Genesis 11:31 we read: "And Terah took his son Abram and his grandson Lot, the son of Haran, and his daughter-in-law Sarai, his son Abram's wife, and they went out with them from Ur of the Chaldees to go to the land of Canaan; and they came to Haran and dwelt there." It seems clear that the events described in this verse follow after the call spoken of in Acts 7:2 and Hebrews 11:8. He had heard the call and believed—yet Terah, we are told, took him out. That was the size of Abraham's faith at the beginning. He left his country, but he left only part of his extended family and none of his father's house. It was his father who led him forth. We do not know how it happened, but the one who was not called became the one who led out, and the one who was called out became the follower.

Noah took his family into the ark with him—his wife, his sons and his sons' wives, all of them. He was told to do so; and what he did was right, for the situation there was different. The ark typifies salvation, and God's salvation is designed to embrace every individual human. The more there are who come into Christ by faith, the happier we ought to be. But Abraham's bringing with him (or accompanying) his parents and their grandson Lot was wrong. For here it was not a matter of amassing individuals for salvation. Abraham was called to be *himself* a chosen vessel in relation to God's purpose, a purpose designed to bring blessing to all the families of the earth. There was no way of taking with him into this purpose others who were not so chosen. Abraham believed, but his understanding was faulty and therefore his faith was deficient. In other words, he was not an exceptional believer; he was just like us!

But Abraham was taken by his father only a part of the way to Canaan; then the movement stopped. "They came to Haran and dwelt there." He had heard God's call, but he did not appreciate the goal to which that call was leading, and so he saw no reason to pay such a price of loneliness. This explains why *we* murmur when God deals with *us*. Remember again, this is not the history of how a man was saved but how he became a vessel for noble use. A valuable vessel or a well-finished tool cannot be created without a high price being paid. Only poor quality goods can be produced cheaply. Let us not misunderstand God's dealings with us. Through Abraham God wanted to introduce a whole new economy in His relations with man, but Abraham did not yet appreciate this fact. Nor do we know what God wants to do with *us*. If He uses special trials and testings it is surely for a special purpose. If our hope is truly in God, there is no need for us to ask why.

So Abraham "came out of the land of the Chaldeans and dwelt in Haran." He thought it quite sufficient to go only half way. Yet the time in Haran was time wasted. Terah means "delay," "duration." The years of Terah's life ran out and they were years in which God did nothing.

Then, when Abraham was already seventy-five years old, there came to him God's second call. "Get out of your country, from your family and from your father's house, to a land that I will show you" (Genesis 12:1). Abraham had shown himself less than thorough in his obedience so far, but God—praise His name!—did not let go His hold upon this man. "From there, when his father was dead, God moved him to this land in which you now dwell" (Acts 7:4). With tears we thank God for that. In Haran everything comes to a standstill, but nothing is more precious than the divine persistence. That is why we are Christians today; that is why we continue. God's patient persistence with Abraham brought him to Canaan. Do not let us be ashamed to admit that in this life of call and response, nothing is of ourselves, all is of God. We would stay on in Haran forever, but the divine perseverance would not let go of us. What amazing grace, that Abraham could still become "the father of all those who believe," even after the wasted years at Haran!

"Then Abram took Sarai his wife and Lot his brother's son, and all their possessions that they had gathered, and the people whom they had acquired in Haran, and they departed to go to the land of Canaan. So they came to the land of Canaan" (Genesis 12:5). God had said, "Come to a land that I will show you" (Acts 7:3), and now at last he arrived. Abraham's coming into the land was of great significance. It was not a question of his owning a piece of territory, for in fact he owned none, but of the power of God taking possession of the whole land of Canaan. And where God's power took possession, there Abraham had his inheritance.

And so it is with us today; for this is the point, that *our inheritance is the ground we take and hold for God now.* We are called by God to a given situation, to maintain there the sovereign rule of heaven, and where the kingdom of heaven is thus effective, there is our inheritance. This is the sorrow of our day, that God's people do not know how to maintain God's power on the earth. They know individual salvation, but they do not know the government of God. And yet our inheritance is bound up with this; we cannot separate our inheritance from God's power. Unless God's rule is established and His enemies are overthrown, we have no inheritance. Remember Samson's riddle: "Out of the eater came something to eat, and out of the strong came something sweet" (Judges 14:14). It is when the lion is slain that we discover the honey.

"The kingdom of heaven" means that, on the one hand, God is King. Despite all appearance to the contrary, He has dominion on the earth. And on the other hand it means that He is ours. This God is our God forever and ever. Do we know what it is to affirm this fact today, by faith, here in the place where He has set us?

"Abram passed through the land to the place of Shechem, as far as the terebinth tree of Moreh. And the Canaanites were then in the land" (12:6). These place-names are interesting. Shechem means "a shoulder," and may contain the idea of obedience. Moreh means "a teacher" and suggests understanding and knowledge. How striking it is that these two ideas should be brought together here in the record, for Jesus Himself said, "If anyone wills to do His will, he shall know" (John 7:17). All knowledge is the outcome of obedience; everything else is just information. It is when we do His will that we *see* His will. Abraham had arrived in the land, and now he began to know why.

For here the Lord appeared to him, assuring him that he was on the right road. "To your descendants I will give this land," He said. This entire land, no less, was his inheritance. Now for the first time we are told that Abraham sacrificed, building an altar to the Lord who had appeared to him. These altars are altars of burnt offering, not of sin offering. They represent Abraham's total committal of himself to God. A man cannot do that until he has first seen Him. But as was true of Abraham, to see him once is enough. It draws out from us everything we have.

Abraham did not come to rest at Shechem. "And he moved from there to the mountain east of Bethel, and he pitched his tent with Bethel on the west and Ai on the east; there he built an altar to the LORD and called on the name of the LORD" (12:8). Here is a second altar. Abraham built the first on his arrival in Canaan, when he saw God, understood, and gave himself. The second he built in the place where he pitched his tent, the place which he made his dwelling-place. In doing so he confessed that God had brought him to rest here.

After his visit to Egypt he came back to this second altar. There was the place where God wanted him to be. It was a token of the eventual accomplishment of all God's purpose.

His tent was pitched between Bethel and Ai. Again the two place-names are significant. Bethel means "the house of God"; Ai means "a heap of ruins." His dwelling lay between them, with Bethel to the west and Ai to the east. Remember that later on in Israel's history the tabernacle of the testimony opened eastward, so that a man entering it faced west. Here at Abraham's dwelling-place if a man faced toward the house of God his back was toward a heap of ruins.

This has a lesson for us. Ai reminds us that the old creation is under judgment. Bethel, not Ai, is the place where Abraham dwells (13:3), the place where through him the power of God will be felt throughout the land. And Bethel is the house of God, or in New Testament terms, the Church, the Body of Christ. Individuals cannot bring to bear upon the earth the sovereign rule of heaven; only the Body, the fellowship of believers in Christ, can do this. But to come to this we must leave behind us that heap of ruins! We bring the kingdom of heaven into this earth only when our natural strength has been brought to nought at the cross and we are living by the common life of the one new man in Christ. This is the witness of Canaan.

4

The Committed Life

THROUGH the period from Adam to Abraham God spoke to men. We are not told, however, that He appeared to them. His first appearance was to Abraham in Mesopotamia (Acts 7:2). God was there laying claim to a man. This was a fresh move on His part; and here in Canaan is another. In the Flood God had judged the whole world; He had not touched and claimed any land for Himself. But now in Abraham He has got the man of His choice *in the land of His choice*, and so now He appears to him here.

At the time when this man was called out of Ur of the Chaldees, the state of things in the world as a whole had become so bad it could not easily have been worse. Through the long years only Enoch had been translated. Out of the disaster of the Flood one family alone had been saved alive. Now in Abraham's world things were no better. The ark had not failed, but the family who were saved had done so. The outcome of that generation was the conspiracy at Babel, and then world-wide idolatry.

But God was not defeated. He had not failed, however much it might seem as though He had. After all this, He—the God of glory—revealed Himself. For He is Omega as well as Alpha. He outlasts and transcends all human failure. Nothing is more stable, more enduring than the glory of God. Man's glory fades and fails; His is unfailing and unfading. There is no way of thwarting God. He cannot be defeated. After two thousand years of the world's sin (or however long the period may have been) He is revealed as still the God of glory! There is always new hope in Him.

Abraham was the first "friend of God." He had a share in God's thoughts. God not only revealed Himself to Abraham but also shared His plans with him—made known to him His intentions. "I am not going to work a sudden miracle from heaven; I shall work through *you*."

This astounding plan of God's must have been most difficult for Abraham to grasp. For us it is not too difficult to understand the fact of personal salvation, to appreciate that God has come so far at so great a cost to rescue us in our state of extreme need; but when it comes to the matter of God's purpose, our finite minds are just not big enough to grasp it. So here we find that God not only showed Himself to Abraham but also spoke to him in clear terms. He told Abraham explicitly what He was going to do.

Nor is it easy to forget God's saving grace when once we have received it; but it is quite easy to lose again the vision of God's eternal purpose. We experience no difficulty at all in losing sight of what God wants us to do! Just a little over-work—indeed we might say, just a little extra work *for God*—is all too capable of diverting our eyes from that ultimate vision. That is why God not only appeared again to Abraham but also *spoke* to him again. Praise Him, He often does that!

For Abraham had seen the vision and, however belatedly, had obeyed the call. God was determined now that he should not lose sight of the hope of God's calling. Therefore at Shechem God appeared to him for the second time, and spoke to him once more. And the message was brief and to the point. "To your descendants I will give this land" (Genesis 12:7).

The promise was for the land. For the earth had been lost; that was the problem. Right down to our day, "the whole world lies under the sway of the wicked one" (1 John 5:19). Now God had begun His movement to deal with this problem. He was claiming, first of all, a land in which to fulfill His will. Secondly, in that land He wanted a people, for a witness.

"Witness" is not the dissemination of what is already general knowledge. We do not witness to what everybody already knows, but to what only a few know concerning the truth. This is the meaning of "witness," and because of conditions generally in the then-world, God wanted within it a witness—a land and a people of His own. Afterward, through them, He would bring the good tidings of His sovereign rule to the whole earth and all the nations.

It is when we see Abraham's call that we see something of the Church's responsibility, for we are Abraham's seed, heirs according to the promise (Galatians 3:29). Our commission is the same as his. Unclouded fellowship and faithful preaching and beautiful Christian lives are not enough. There must be witness. The Church is a golden candlestick, not an ornamental vase. Nor is it enough that it should be of gold; it must be a candlestick. The light of God must shine forth from it.

In Canaan Abraham went through three tests and he built three altars. As we have seen, the first altar was in Shechem (Genesis 12:7) and the second at Bethel (12:8; 13:4). Then he went south to Egypt, fell into sin, and at length returned again to Bethel. The third altar he built was at Hebron (13:18). These are the three special points of Canaan in God's eyes. Each was sanctified by an altar. What they are, Canaan is. God has no use for a place where there is no altar. "I will give you this land—Shechem, Bethel, Hebron." They are Canaan. Let us look at them now more closely.

The name Shechem, we have said, means "a shoulder." It is the place of greatest strength, for that is the meaning of "shoulder" in Hebrew. Canaan is not only a land of plenty and of milk-and-honey sweetness, it is the place of God's own strength—the place of victory, where enemies are cast out and kept out. Its strength is a *living* strength. The well of Sychar is in Shechem, a figure of the power of the living Christ in His people. The Lord's own life is manifest there, and none go away empty. "Whoever drinks of the water that I shall give him will never thirst. But the water that I shall give him will become in him a fountain of water springing up into everlasting life" (John 4:14). Those who are always empty, always thirsty, always seeking for this or that, never satisfied, are weak and of little use to God. It is the satisfied who are strong, and God has made provision that we should all be satisfied. He offers us such satisfaction in His Son that we are able to say, "I want nothing, I need nothing for myself." That is strength. Is it not true that our greatest weakness as Christians arises from within, because we are unsatisfied, or dissatisfied? Shechem and the land of Canaan imply satisfaction, full and complete, and that means strength.

Neither the world nor the powers of darkness can find an entry there.

Moreh, we have said, means "a teacher" and implies knowledge. Knowledge is the fruit of strength. For Moreh was the name of a terebinth or oak tree in Shechem, and a tree grows out of the earth upon which it stands. Knowledge comes from, and is the fruit of, strength and satisfaction, not of doctrine. The weakness of today's knowledge is that it is mere information. Without the strength of the Lord satisfying us and producing knowledge, we have no knowledge at all. The vessel God wants for His work is not prepared by hearing a lot of things, but by seeing and receiving and being satisfied. Its understanding is based on the life of Christ within, not on information about Him. We must beware of just passing on to others what we hear. No matter how precious or profound the teaching may be, we are not to be disseminators of information. In this respect people with good memories can be most dangerous. To prattle on about divine things will achieve nothing, and may take us far from the will of God. God's power on earth cannot be maintained by what we hear but only by our knowledge of Him. What must characterize the Christian Church is what we know within us. God deliver us from a merely intellectual gospel!

Why was Bethel necessary as well as Shechem? Because in spite of Shechem, in spite of their knowledge of life in Christ and their satisfaction with that life, men are still independent and individualistic. And God does not want a heap but a house. God is a God of order, and in God's purpose there must be the order of the Body of Christ. Christ as a Son must be over His house, whose house we are (Hebrews 3:6).

There is much in the world that goes by the name of the house of God. The great historic churches and denominations all claim that title. Some are false houses, based on wrong principles of authority and built largely of dead bricks and not of living stones. The Protestant church, in as far as it is evangelical, has more life. In it are many living stones, but they are individual and not united. Liberty of conscience is its speciality. There is much splendid material, but it is not built into a house.

But quietly, in many places and largely unseen, God is raising up a vessel which is truly His house. It consists not of single outstanding individuals, whether great in preaching or revival or anything else, but in humble men and women who have been welded into one by the cross. Shechem must become Bethel. God must deliver us from the whole principle of individualism. He must save us from wanting to be outstanding individual Christians, and somehow make us one in His house. For it is the house of God that is His witness in the earth. Everyone knows how difficult it is for Christians to live together! When by the grace of God it happens, and continues to happen, even hell takes notice.

But let us be careful. Is God's house a principle to be followed, or a life to be lived? Is it something to copy, or something to be? It would be easy, having seen the value of life together, to determine at all costs to apply the principles by which it should work. But this would not achieve the result. We must have the life of the Body, the shared life of Christ that comes from Him as Head, before we can abide by its principles. They cannot just be learned.

Then how is this shared life attained? Our tent must be pitched, as we have seen already, between Ai and Bethel, between the heap and the house. On the one hand there is the house of God, the testimony to God's authority and rule in the earth. On the other hand there is the heap of ruins, the ruin of our hopes and our ambitions, our expectations and our self-esteem. Only if our back is to this are we facing that. This is both a geographical and a spiritual fact. Only if we have accepted God's judgment upon the old creation as final are we facing toward what is represented by Bethel. When our flesh, our natural strength, has been dealt with, then, and only then, do we fit into God's house naturally and without effort. We are as living stones, just the right size and shape for the place He has for us. Otherwise, however much we try to fit ourselves in, we just belong on the heap.

Many of us, alas, have little idea of what it means to have our natural strength judged and dealt with. Rather do we boast about it. "I feel this." "I look at it this way." "In my humble opinion. . . ." Secretly we glory in our opinions and in our difference from and independence of others, and we never really recognize this as outright defeat. Those who have not seen themselves by nature judged and cast upon that heap of ruins have not found their place in the Church, nor heard the voice of God there. May God have mercy on us when we dare to think that the Church of God is wrong and we are right. It is not just His people that we are repudiating in doing so, but God Himself, who pleases to reveal Himself among them.

Oh, you say, all this talk about our old nature being dealt with at the cross of Christ is excellent, but it is rather negative. Now tell us the positive side! Let me reply quite simply that the positive side is just a matter of life—spontaneous, miraculous life. The child who is born does not have to worry where his life comes from; he just lives it quite naturally. The believer who is born again does not have to puzzle out how his new life works. It comes from Christ; he has it, he rejoices in it, and quite naturally and spontaneously he lives it. And the believer who has seen that the life of Christ is a shared life of which *all* His own partake—he is in just the same position. He accepts the fact and thanks God, and the life flows. There is an altar at Bethel, and God receives what is offered, namely, our acceptance of Christ as our shared life. We may in our folly depart into Egypt, but God will bring us back there.

The principles of life together will follow. Abraham moved on to Hebron (13:18), and there built his third altar. Hebron means "a league." In New Testament terms we could substitute the word "fellowship," and certainly it is in fellowship together that the fact of the shared life of Christians is put to the proof. Bethel represents the life in the Body of Christ; Hebron represents the principle of living that life. The first must precede the second, and there is no way of getting to Hebron but through Bethel. You cannot take a group of men and put God's principles of fellowship into it. Fellowship in Christ is a quite natural, effortless thing because it stems from the fact of the living Body of Christ, and there is therefore no need to plan or organize it. It flows spontaneously when our hearts are, as was Abraham's, given "to the LORD."

It is a matter of experience that we cannot go on indefinitely, nor can we witness effectively, without fellowship. God often brings the most spiritually mature people up against a blank wall in order to teach them this. They reach an impasse, something they cannot deal with alone. Then they discover the absolute necessity of fellowship with others in Christ, and learn the practical values of the corporate life. But when once this is known, there is a new fruitfulness. At Hebron Abraham dwelt by the terebinths of Mamre. Mamre means "firmness" or "vigor." When, like Abraham, the people of God are firmly established here, then indeed they have a witness. The events that immediately follow show how mighty was Abraham's witness to the world once he had come to Hebron.

The linking factor in these three places is Abraham's "altar to the LORD" (12:7, 12:8, 13:18). At the altar, in principle, God accepts only Christ. We, in making our own "living sacrifice" (Romans 12:1), affirm that we accept Christ for ourselves, and accordingly God can receive us in Him. Because we have each abandoned any expectation in our self, and are looking to His Son Jesus Christ for everything, God accepts completely what we offer. Upon that basis, together we witness.

5

The Man in the Land

FELLOWSHIP is something we should prize highly because God prizes it highly. If there is life in me and not merely pretense, and if the same is true of my fellow believers, then, however simple they may be, when I meet them I should encounter life in them—and encountering it, I should appreciate it. We must learn to value our fellow Christians and not engage in fault-finding or in exposing their weaknesses. For did not Jesus Himself show infinite patience with men, suffering much at their hands? Even His own disciples often put His self-restraint severely to the test.

As the Son over God's house, the Lord Jesus not only offers us strength and knowledge; He has set us also an example of submission and restraint. He was ever the Son, learning obedience to His Father by the things which He suffered; and He was ever the Servant, who, when He was reviled, did not revile in return; when He suffered, He did not threaten (Hebrews 5:8; 1 Peter 2:23).

In relation to the land of Canaan which was to be Israel's inheritance, Abraham was put to the test on three separate occasions. For he was a very ordinary man, just like you and me, whom God had selected and set apart for this special task—and his faith was no greater than ours. So the tests he went through brought him discipline at the hands of varied kinds of people, and they are just the kind of experiences we go through.

Abraham's first test occurred not long after his arrival in Canaan, and soon after he had sacrificed at Bethel. He journeyed on toward the South, and when conditions became difficult through famine he arrived at length in Egypt. There he found himself in an embarrassing situation, and there he sinned by practicing deception, with the result that he was severely rebuked by Pharaoh. He, a believer, was taken to task by a man of the world!

This test really turned on the question of the land. How truly did Abraham want "this land" (12:7)? God had given it to him, but he had not yet realized the importance of keeping it—of staying on there. For him it was to be "the land of your sojournings," and as such, his everlasting possession (17:8). But Abraham had not yet come to value it. God had still to establish him there. It is one thing to have the fullness of God as a gift, but quite another to be established in it.

In Egypt Abraham learned that there was no land like the land of Canaan. In Canaan he had had no need to side-step danger by the exercise of his wits and at the cost of rebuke by an unbeliever. Here in Egypt he found himself doing just that, and knew he had only himself to blame. He had landed himself in this trouble and he saw the wrong of it. He accepted the rebuff, even at the hands of a pagan monarch, and as quickly as possible he returned to Bethel.

Abraham had learned his first lesson, namely, that the land was precious. Now his second test arrived, and it was of a different character. Lot was still with him—Lot who had come as a kind of passenger on this journey of faith, and who would, after his death, leave behind him two of Israel's worst enemies. Here in Canaan Abraham and his nephew had begun to prosper, and soon the grazing land was not extensive enough to support their combined flocks and herds. Because of the prevailing congestion, their servants began to fight.

In the matter of leaving his family, Abraham had never fully obeyed. He still held on to Lot. Now at last it became clear that, through Lot, God was disciplining him. He came to see that God's purpose concerned him alone, and did not include Lot. We can lead men into salvation. We cannot, however, lead them into the calling and the service of God, for this is a personal thing. Abraham recognized this, and now at length he proposed to Lot that their ways should part.

But we have just seen that Abraham had already learned his first lesson, which was that to him this land was of priceless worth. Surely then, if it was so precious, it ought to be held on to. Should he not keep it for himself, and send Lot back to Haran? No, he would give this younger man every chance to find the way of God *for himself.* So he showed him the whole land and offered him his choice.

Thus, on the one hand, Abraham perfected his obedience by separating from his nephew; on the other, he learned not to maintain his rights to the land by selfish, grasping methods. He was not to hold on to it for personal ends. The land was God's, not his.

Here is a most important lesson. We must learn to trust God to keep for us what He gives us, and must never seek to possess it by worldly means. Because we stand upon the earth for God, we are not therefore to become earthly. This land was God's gift to Abraham. To know this fact, and yet, knowing it, to let it all go and leave the outcome to God—this is the work of the cross in a man.

Lot chose the richest portion, and Abraham let him have it without demur, but it left Abraham still dwelling in the highlands of Canaan. Lot had not usurped his inheritance, for in the outcome the plain was divinely excluded from it. Those who know God have no need to protect their rights. Because they believe in Him, they learn to bear the cross daily and to rely upon Him for the outcome.

Abraham had advanced to this point in obedience and self-restraint, and now at this juncture God spoke to him again. "The LORD said to Abram, after Lot had separated from him: 'Lift your eyes and look from the place where you are—northward, southward, eastward and westward; for all the land which you see I give to you and your descendants forever. And I will make your descendants as the dust of the earth; so that if a man could number the dust of the earth, then your descendants could also be numbered. Arise, walk in the land through its length and its width, for I give it to you'" (13:14–17). Abraham had obeyed in the matter of Lot, and once again God established him in the land with not one whit of the promised territory diminished. It always pays to put things back into God's hands, for our battle is spiritual and not carnal. What God gives, He gives. There is no need to protect it ourselves. If we grip a thing tightly, we lose it. Not until we seem to have lost it altogether do we really have it.

With this test passed, God had a basis in Abraham for fellowship, and as we saw, Abraham moved his tent and came and dwelt at Hebron. He did so without harboring any reproach in his heart for Lot. It would have been easy to let Lot go but nevertheless hope that his conscience would trouble him. It might have seemed fitting, and even necessary, to say at least, "God will judge you." We may reach the point of letting go of the land but still not find it easy to let our brother go without rebuking him. Yet God required such a humble spirit if Abraham was to come to Hebron—with all that Hebron means. He is perfect in His dealings with His own.

Abraham's third test, and the last connected with the land itself, is of course the battle of the kings. Sodom, where Lot now dwelt, was raided, and Lot himself was carried off. Abraham went at once, with all his tiny forces, to his nephew's rescue.

How tempting it would have been to say, "You should have known! It is your own fault." But even after Lot's departure, and his selfish and disastrous choice of Sodom as a dwelling-place, he is still to Abraham a "brother" (14:14). Abraham was a true overcomer; he had conquered himself first of all. In him was no selfish individualism. He was still in Hebron, the place of fellowship, and all were his brothers—even Lot, who lived for nothing and no one but himself. Only those standing in the position represented by Hebron can, like Abraham, wage spiritual warfare.

Lot was not changed at all as a result of being rescued from the kings; he went right back to Sodom. But victory was not a question of whether or not a change was wrought in Lot, but of the overthrow of those kings. Their power was broken; that was what mattered. We are not to worry about whether the brethren are "improved" by the experience, so long as the enemy is defeated. That man in trouble is a brother; I love him in the Lord. However much he may in the past have injured me, I will still love and pray for him, and I will help him now. Here for the first time the character of Abraham really shines forth. May God teach us the lesson that he displays.

For it is so easy to conquer, and in conquering to rescue others, and having done so to be proud or self-righteous about it. "Didn't I tell you so!" we say sourly, or we look around for some reward, some congratulation, some coveted honor. So it is not surprising that this test includes another, a subsidiary one.

On his return from the discomfiture of the raiders, Abraham was met by the king of Sodom himself, who came out to him offering a very generous reward, namely, all the goods recovered. But Abraham had already learned that his resources lay elsewhere. His benefactor was in heaven. He maintained his clear stand therefore that, apart from God, no one could give him anything. This shows what a truly great thing God had done in him. We may stand in the position God has given and know assuredly that none can hurt us; but do we believe that none could help us either, unless God sends them? Abraham had demonstrated the one; now he confidently affirmed the other. "I have raised my hand to the LORD, God Most High, the Possessor of heaven and earth, that I will take nothing, from a thread to a sandal strap, and that I will not take anything that is yours, lest you should say, 'I have made Abram rich'" (14:22–23).

That title, "God Most High, Possessor of heaven and earth," is most striking in this setting, and especially its last two words. It has just previously been used for the first time on the lips of Melchizedek, king of Salem. Now it is Abraham's testimony. The earth is the Lord's. Melchizedek had forestalled the king of Sodom and had come out to meet Abraham, not on the mountain but in the valley—the place of testing. He had come to him with bread and wine, the bread of heaven (John 6) and the new wine of the kingdom (John 2). These represent our complete satisfaction with Christ Himself, and Abraham met the king of Sodom as a satisfied man. Earth was under the curse, and Sodom itself might be earth's darkest place, but Abraham could proclaim God as Possessor of heaven *and earth*. God had obtained a man in the land! This was what made it possible.

That tremendous fact brings to a conclusion this section of the story in which the land is in question. At the risk of his life Abraham had overcome the invading kings and had rescued Lot. Thereupon his real motives had been put to the test. You cannot stand and fight for God if there is one scrap of worldly scheming or planning or ambition left in you. It is only when the world has lost its power to touch you that you can do this. To have yielded to the king of Sodom would have been a greater moral overthrow than to have failed to go out after the raiding kings. But for Abraham the question was already settled, and God had His man where He needed him. Abraham in the land could begin to claim the earth for God.

No wonder God speaks to Abraham again. "After these things the word of the LORD came to Abram in a vision, saying, 'Do not be afraid, Abram. I am your shield, your exceedingly great reward'" (15:1). He speaks to comfort and reassure Abraham. Why is this necessary for such an outstanding man of faith? Because Abraham was still a man, and his victory was a human one, not a superhuman one. Immediately after receiving the bread and wine it may have seemed to him easy to refuse the reward offered by the king of Sodom. Home again, however, away from the excitement of the great occasion, he would begin to think of the many enemies he might have made. Whenever God says "Do not be afraid" it is because there is cause for fear. "I am your shield"—none can touch you. "I am your reward"—and "reward" here is not an object but a title of God Himself. Yes, I am enough. All you have lost you have in Me—and more!

But Abraham came back with a reply. "My problem is not as simple as that! Lord, don't you understand? It is not just that I fear those kings or grudge that reward. It is the question of a *son*. Nothing is any use unless I have a *son*." One can sense Abraham's agony of heart in his double appeal to the Lord. "Abram said, 'Lord GOD, what will You give me, seeing I go childless, and the heir of my house is Eliezer of Damascus? . . . Look, You have given me no offspring; indeed, one born in my house [a servant in my household—NIV] is my heir!'" (15:2–3).

Did not God know that Abraham wanted a son? Of course He did; but there is something very significant here. For God wants you and me to be in a true sense His friends— to enter into His thoughts, to ask Him intelligently for that which He longs to give. Abraham knew that God's plan on earth could not be accomplished unless he himself had a son. He must have an heir by birth and not by purchase, a son and not a servant. God had shown him this, and now, he in turn told God what must be done! This is friendship.

God answered him with a very firm assurance. "One who will come from your own body shall be your heir." He brought him out under the sky and He said, "Look now toward heaven, and count the stars if you are able to number them. So shall your descendants be." And now we are told, "He believed in the LORD; and He accounted it to him for righteousness" (15:6). Here is the first direct mention of faith.

It is, we saw, a fundamental fact that God's purpose is fulfilled only through those who are born of God. God wants a company of those who have looked toward heaven and believed, but He is content to begin with one. Abraham had been shown the fullness of the Lord's purpose and his heart had responded. In him God had His beginning!

Now once more God affirmed that His purpose with Abraham was in relation to the land. "I am the LORD, who brought you out of Ur of the Chaldees, to give you this land to inherit it." And Abraham came back with the question: "Lord GOD, how shall I know that I will inherit it?" (15:7–8). It was not unbelief; he wanted to understand more, and on our behalf he was asking the way to the inheritance. There follows the incident of Abraham's vigil over the offering, and his vision during a deep sleep. The essence of God's answer was that Abraham's inheritance was where God's power operated. The way was the pathway of the cross, the way of death. The sacrificial animals were to be divided. The recovery of the earth depended upon the laying down of a life. We cannot overemphasize the cross of Christ. For Him it meant the laying down of His own life on our behalf, and until the cross has worked in us too, and our lives have been laid down, we cannot stand victorious in the land. We cannot be soldiers of the cross unless the cross has first done its work in us.

In the work of God it is not sufficient for us as young people to be zealous, to be good preachers of the gospel and to know our Bibles well. God wants clean vessels, not big or clever or efficient instruments. God wants purity, not mixture (see James 3:8–12). The messages God can use through His servants are not the impressive, specially prepared ones, but those that spring from and are backed by a life that is pure. For this we must know the values of the cross. It is the death of Christ working in a man's life that produces such purity of spirit. And purity brings light.

Abraham experienced "horror and great darkness" (15:12). When we see the holy purpose to which we are called, and then look upon ourselves, we too are utterly undone. Recall Peter's dismay when he saw the catch of fishes. Falling down at Jesus' knees, "Depart from me," he cried, "for I am a sinful man, O Lord!" (Luke 5:8). To know as a fact that the work is too sacred for me to touch—that is the beginning of my usefulness. The road thither may be a road through death, but it is a road with Christ, and it leads to "great possessions" (Genesis 15:14).

6

The Heir and
the Proof of Time

BY THE TIME we reach chapter 15 of Genesis a new idea has come into the forefront of the narrative. The land is still in view, with all that that signifies of God's claim to have a kingdom on the earth, but from now onward attention centers on the son, expressed in the term "your offspring," or, literally, "your seed." The Hebrew word is *zera*. Abraham's problem, seeing he is childless, is, who is to *inherit* this land? "Look, You have given me no offspring; indeed, one born in my house is my heir."

"This one shall not be your heir," replied the Lord. "One who will come from your own body shall be your heir. Look now toward heaven, and count the stars if you are able to number them. So shall your descendants be." And then it is said of Abraham that "he believed in the LORD, and He accounted it to him for righteousness."

Now when we come to the letter to the Galatians and this passage is dealt with, the apostle Paul makes the point that God speaks of "your seed," using a singular noun. The promises were to Abraham and his seed. "He does not say, 'And to seeds,' as of many, but as of one, 'And to your Seed,' who is Christ" (Galatians 3:16). The promise pointed not only to Isaac but to Jesus Christ. The one son, Isaac, is the heir—yes, but in the long term it is Christ who is to have the land. He alone has the strength to take and keep it for God. He is the one who does God's work of recovery. This gives an altogether deeper meaning to the promise to Abraham of an heir, for "when the fullness of the time had come, God sent forth His Son" (Galatians 4:4). Without Him the whole plan would collapse.

Nevertheless it is also true that Abraham's seed are to be countless as the stars. "For you are all sons of God through faith in Christ Jesus. And if you are Christ's, then you are Abraham's seed, heirs according to the promise" (Galatians 3:26, 29). Today, we who believe owe everything to Christ; and yet in another sense we stand in the position of Abraham. As His Church we are called by God to bring Christ into His inheritance in the land. The question with Abraham was, Could he become God's vessel to bring in Isaac? And it is the same question today: Can the Church become God's vessel to bring Christ into His place? The Church counts for nothing in herself, except as a vessel to bring in Christ. God's purpose is in the Son.

But how, we ask ourselves, can we become such a vessel, to give God's Son the opportunity to display His power in the great work of recovery? Abraham, we find, underwent three further tests, this time in relation to his own son, to prepare him for this very task. In these three lie the answers to that question. We shall look now at the first of them.

In relation to the son, Abraham's first test was the test of time. As we have seen in Genesis 15:4, God had promised him an heir. The time went by, Abraham, we are told, had believed; but he was not superhuman, and his faith was still in the process of developing.

At the age of eighty-five, he had been in the land for ten years (16:3). He felt it was time his son arrived, if he was going to have one at all. So he adopted Sarah's suggestion and took her maidservant, Hagar, to be a second wife. Hagar's son was born when Abraham was eighty-six.

What he did not know was that God had planned for him to have a son by Sarah when he himself was one hundred. Instead, he had Ishmael fourteen years earlier. So we can say that Abraham was defeated in his first test. He had not seen that to exercise faith is to *cease striving*. He believed, but he thought he must help God, and that in taking Hagar he was insuring that her child should be the fulfillment of God's promise. There were many things he knew he could not do, but surely he could do this, for this was what God wanted!

What Abraham overlooked was that this matter of the son went deeper than the mere question of *his* having one. What was vital was *from whom* the son came—*who* gave him? It is not a question of whether we are active or not, but of who originates the actions and whose power is behind them! Unless Abraham's son was God's gift, what use was he to God?

Is it wrong to help people? No, but we need to be sure that the help they receive is help from *God*. Is it wrong to preach the Good News? Certainly not! But the question is, who is doing it? Is the word preached God's word? God does not only want right things done; he wants us to be the medium of right things that *He* is doing. The *source* of the action, not just the activity itself, is the important thing. A thing may even be God's will, just as it was certainly God's will that Abraham should have a son; nevertheless what matters is *who* is doing that will.

All Abraham got for his efforts was Ishmael. True, Abraham was intended to be a father; but this meant essentially that he was to discover the meaning of the word "father" by learning the fundamental lesson that everything comes from *God* as Father. Only so would he himself be worthy to be the father of those who believe. The source is everything because it is the source that gets the credit. What I do, I get credit for; after all, it is I who did it! So after a piece of service, however fruitful, the ultimate question is not "What are the results?" but "Lord, *who* has done this?— you or I?" No matter how expertly we may do it, we shall invite not praise but rebuke from God. Purity or otherwise in our work depends on how much of God and how much of ourselves there is in it. If we are truly God's servants we know perfectly well that we get no peace or joy from what we have done by striving. When He quietly puts us aside, we praise Him because what has been done is something we have had no part in. The origin was God Himself.

I am afraid this is not a popular thing to speak of. Preach to stir men to more evangelizing, more activity, more sacrifice, and they will listen and agree. But talk about the worthlessness of our work for God, even when it is not sinfully but well done, and we meet disapproval and misunderstanding.

Yet this is the central point in service. Whether we can bring in Christ to be God's vessel of recovery depends on whether we can get out of the way to make room for Him. Nothing—good work, service, preaching the Word, even doing His will—can satisfy His heart if *we* are the source of it. Only what He does in us and through us can satisfy Him.

We watch a child making models out of mud. He may have real imagination and produce some quite recognizable models, but we say, "They are nothing but mud. It is only childish play." Yet the difference between that child and ourselves is very trifling compared with the difference between ourselves and God. He is *God*. We are *men*. He uses us—and rejoices to use us—as His instruments, but that is all. *He* uses us.

In Galatians the apostle Paul draws an interesting parallel with this passage. Hagar, he says, represents "the Law." The Ten Commandments are, of course, ten things that God requires. In Abraham too we have a man seeking to give God what He requires; he has set out to please God. Yet those who do so, Paul says, put themselves under a curse (Galatians 3:10). The only effect, therefore, of Abraham's good works is that Ishmael is born "according to the flesh" (4:29).

God had said that the son would be Sarah's. Isaac was the child of promise (4:28), a work of God's grace. And grace is God working instead of me. When God worked, Isaac was born "according to the Spirit." At eighty-six Abraham's natural strength had been still there. At one hundred "his body was as good as dead" (Romans 4:19, asv). There was no longer any way for him to have a son naturally. *Then* Isaac came. We too need to reckon ourselves dead before we can believe fully in the God who gives life to the dead.

Abraham was shown that he himself was not the father, the source, of anything. God waits until we have reached an end of ourselves, and then Isaac comes. There is something of the atmosphere of Genesis 1 here. There is no other chapter in the Bible like that one. "God saw everything that He had made, and indeed it was very good."

With Isaac it was altogether a matter of time—God's time. We often think it would be good if we could start work for Him sooner, but when we know Him, we know what it is to wait for God's time. It is Isaac, not Ishmael, who is the one to fulfill God's purpose and maintain His witness in the earth. Not only was Ishmael valueless to God, none have so injured God's people and their witness, or so fought against God Himself, as has Ishmael. To try to help God can be to injure His work.

There may be many Ishmaels, but there is only one Isaac. We can bring Ishmael on the scene at any time; there is only one time for Isaac—God's time. Shall we decide to wait for Isaac, or shall we determine to have Ishmael in his place? Any time is convenient for Ishmael.

For God to have complete dominion over us means coming to the extreme end of ourselves. And yet to know that God has spoken through us Himself, even once, is better than a lifetime of our own service. Don't compare yourself with others. Recognize one thing only, the difference between man's work and God's. It is a question of source, and it is a question of time. If God sets us aside even for three months, we cannot bear it. Yet Abraham had to wait for his son fifteen years.

Before Abraham was eighty-five his faith was far from perfect. Yet we read that he exercised this deficient faith:

"He believed in the LORD; and He accounted it to him for righteousness" (Genesis 15:6). Praise God, he was justified by faith! It is sufficient just to believe. But in the fifteen years that followed he learned some tremendous lessons, and how he glorified God when at length the impossible happened and Isaac was given! Paul says that when Isaac was conceived, Abraham already considered himself "dead" (Romans 4:19). He had given up! The more utter the impossibility of doing a thing ourselves, the more glory we give to Him who does it. And what God does is always "very good."

7

The Covenant of Grace

ONE striking feature marks the thirteen years that followed Ishmael's birth. Throughout them all God did not speak to Abraham. His record is empty. What we have done on our own, God leaves us to get on with; He does not speak. But when Abraham was "dead"—dry and old, and could no longer have a son if he wanted one—*then* God spoke to him.

The starting point of all our progress is in God's gracious call; not in our desires. Abraham had not repented. Rather, Ishmael was growing yearly more precious to him. He had not realized his wrong, nor sought after God. From our standpoint, measuring him by all we have said so far, there was not much hope for him. But his hope was not dependent on whether he wanted God but on the fact that God wanted *him*. God was still at work on him; He had not let him go. If God wants a man, that man cannot escape God's hand. How we need to learn to commit ourselves to the hand of the Almighty God!

So, after these years, God spoke to Abraham again. "When Abram was ninety-nine years old, the LORD appeared to Abram and said to him, 'I am God Almighty; walk before Me and be blameless'" (Genesis 17:1). For the first time God uses the title El Shaddai, "God Almighty." Abraham knew God had power and was mighty, but he did not know Him as *all*-mighty. God said, "Learn this, and be blameless"— that is to say, unblemished by the world.

Now God made a covenant with Abraham. God wanted a people who would spring from Him, and He defines in the terms of the covenant where they must stand in order to be such a people. "I will make My covenant between Me and you, and will multiply you exceedingly. Behold, My covenant is with you, and you shall be a father of many nations. And I will establish My covenant between Me and you and your descendants after you throughout their generations, for an everlasting covenant, to be God to you and your descendants after you" (17:2, 4, 7).

The sign of the covenant was circumcision. They were to be a people with no confidence in the flesh. They must not only be born and called forth by God, they must bear in their flesh His sign. To be born, and to be bought with a price, is not enough. God has redeemed us and begotten us again, but we are still not in the position of God's people, maintaining His witness in the earth, fulfilling His purpose, unless there is effective in us what is meant by circumcision. "You shall be circumcised," runs the command, "and it shall be a sign of the covenant between Me and you." And it continues: "The uncircumcised male . . . shall be cut off from his people; he has broken My covenant" (17:11, 14). Note carefully that those not circumcised were not therefore exterminated (like the people of Canaan), for this is not a question of salvation but of witness only. Their *name* was "cut off." In other words, we may be redeemed and possess new life, but if we do not recognize the cross of Christ as dealing with the flesh in us, we have no name as His witnesses.

What, then, is circumcision? The apostle Paul tells us that in Christ "you were also circumcised with the circumcision made without hands, by putting off the body of the flesh, by the circumcision of Christ" (Colossians 2:11). Elsewhere he says, "We are the circumcision, who worship God in the Spirit, rejoice in Christ Jesus, and have no confidence in the flesh" (Philippians 3:3). And then he goes on to catalog the various grounds he had previously felt *himself* to have for such confidence. They turn out to be things in no way sinful or wrong in themselves. His racial purity, his strict religious upbringing, his sincere zeal for God—these things were not sinful at all. They were simply grounds for natural pride. But "those who are in the flesh cannot please God" (Romans 8:8). The trouble today is that we do not recognize this. Romans chapter 7 is Paul's description of one who is doing his best to please God in the flesh, and it is one big "*cannot.*"

Sin in a man is comparatively easy to deal with. But when it comes to having a part in God's work of recovery, the trouble arises with *the flesh* that wants to please God. It is here that the cross of Christ comes to our aid. It undermines our self-confidence, so that, for example, we can no longer speak as dogmatically as we did, but it gives us a wonderful confidence in God.

It is as though God said to Abraham, "What you need is faith and not works. You tried thirteen years ago; but I promised, not in order that you should bring it about but because *I* intended to bring it about." Circumcision was the sign of that. It is to be a sign, for all generations of God's children, that they know that in the flesh they are helpless.

A sign is a peculiarity. We see it, and by it we recognize a person. What is the distinctive mark of our Christian life before men? Is it wisdom, or honesty? Is it love, or eloquence in the Word of God? No; the feature that distinguishes the people of God is their lack of an overweening self-confidence. Alas, it is a feature hard to find. As young Christians we *know* everything: salvation, the fullness of the Spirit, the will of God! We are quite *sure* we know God's plan for us. But where is the fear and the trembling? Where is the uncertainty that knows it may well be mistaken, and that leans— yes *leans*—on God?

In chapter 15 we read of Abraham that he believed. Now, in chapter 17, the fulfillment of the promise is near; yet it seems that Abraham's faith has dwindled. We are told that he fell on his face and laughed (17:17). It was probably the only position in which he dared laugh! For him and Sarah to have a son now was ridiculous. After all, he was a man of a hundred. He had heard nothing like it. His early faith had been true faith, but even that had had an element of self-confidence in it, and now even his faith was dead! He had not backslidden. This was part of God's work in him. The Father of the faithful has to *lose* his faith! For it had been a mixed faith—in God and in Abraham.

God was bringing about in Abraham a new quality of faith. That laugh was not a laugh at God but a laugh at himself. "And not being weak in faith, he did not consider his own body, already dead (since he was about a hundred years old), and the deadness of Sarah's womb. He did not waver at the promise of God through unbelief, but was strengthened in faith, giving glory to God, and being fully convinced that what He had promised He was able also to perform. And therefore 'it was accounted to him for righteousness'" (Romans 4:19–22). This is true faith. When we are defeated and God does not speak, He is leading us to the end of ourselves and to a complete confidence in Him. There is no substitute for that. We try to help God out, and inflate our faith, and make long prayers, but nothing happens. There is prayer which shows no self-confidence, which cries out in the midst of doubt and fear: "I don't know whether it is any use or not to do so, but *I believe!*" God can use faith that is exercised in the midst of extreme doubt, faith as small as a grain of mustard seed.

With the matter of circumcision settled we move into chapter 18 and find Abraham in the most privileged position of "a friend of God." This is quite the most remarkable chapter in the Old Testament. Abraham is still in Mamre, the place of fullness. Three men come to him, and one of them is God in human form. This occurs in no other place in the Old Testament. God appeared, not as before in glory, but walking, bringing two angels. Abraham recognized Him and addressed Him as "my Lord." He received the three of them as guests, inviting them to rest and wash and eat. This was fellowship and intercourse with God of a new order. As the latter part of the chapter shows, Abraham was taken into the divine counsels to have a part in them. He was God's *friend.*

They talked of Abraham's son, yet to be given. Now it was Sarah who broke into laughter. With Abraham the question was already settled. It was this that had qualified him to be God's friend.

The story of Sodom works itself out, and after that a strange thing happens. Abraham is subjected to his second test with regard to his son. This takes place at Gerar in the land of the Philistines. Here Abraham comes to dwell, and as he did before in Egypt, he tells a lie to Abimelech king of Gerar. After chapter 18 and Abraham's fellowship with God, this is difficult to understand.

But there is a difference here from the incident in chapter 12. For when Abimelech rebukes him, Abraham explains why he did it. It was a thing they had planned together back in Mesopotamia. "We thought God wanted us to move about in this land. We thought you were idolaters, and we were afraid, so we made this plan." The thing had not originated in Egypt: it only came to the surface there. It had its roots in Mesopotamia, and now, here in Gerar it crops up again. Abraham is put to shame. He has to learn that Sarah cannot be separated from him. In Mesopotamia he had thought she could.

Abraham represents faith; Sarah represents grace. It is impossible to separate them. If the one is gone the other is useless. Here was one more treacherous thing that had to be rooted out before Isaac could be given. Faith that does not rest on God's grace is valueless. You cannot sacrifice Sarah.

For Sarah's sake the whole of Abimelech's house was punished (20:17). Abraham was required to pray for them. It cannot possibly have been an easy thing to do. The women of Gerar were barren. How could he pray for them when his own wife had the same trouble? For other things, yes; but how for this?

But he did not ask that question. Now he had completely overcome the fears and questions and doubts that had had their root in Mesopotamia. "My wife is God's affair, and so are theirs. I have no confidence except in God." The lurking fear had been dragged out into the light of day, and slain. He was free to pray for others. He did not pray for Sarah, for now he had no need to. Immediately after this Isaac was conceived. "The LORD visited Sarah as He had said, and the LORD did for Sarah as He had spoken. For Sarah conceived and bore Abraham a son in his old age, at the set time of which God had spoken to him. And Abraham called the name of his son who was born to him—whom Sarah bore to him—Isaac" (Genesis 21:1–3).

8

The Gifts, or the Giver?

ABRAHAM had learned that God is Father. It was this that made possible his prayer for Abimelech's household. He knew that neither their troubles nor Sarah's hindered God in the least. He knew that ultimately fruitfulness depended neither on them nor on himself. It was God's gift. He could not have prayed for the people of Gerar if he had still been nursing hopes in himself in regard to his own need. He prayed a costly prayer, and the price of it was a complete abandonment of himself. It was a prayer God would answer immediately.

To know God in the closest relationship of "our Father" is one thing. To know him as God the Father, the source and originator of everything, is something more. Abraham had learned that nothing could hinder and nothing could help God. He is almighty!

We read now that Sarah saw the son of Hagar the Egyptian mocking, and that she said to Abraham "Cast out this bondwoman and her son; for the son of this bondwoman shall not be heir with my son, namely with Isaac." This appears to be merely human jealousy, but God was speaking through Sarah. This is clear from Galatians 4:30. Ultimately only one son can fulfill God's purpose, namely Christ.

Ishmael represents Adam, the man of the flesh. In him we are in bondage, and Paul says "Stand fast therefore in the liberty by which Christ has made us free, and do not be entangled again with a yoke of bondage" (Galatians 5:1). How, then, are we to act toward the flesh?

Notice, first, that Ishmael was not cast out until after Isaac was born and weaned. It is no use preaching against the flesh to unbelievers. They are flesh, and they possess nothing else! There must be an Isaac, a new birth. When Isaac came into his position and was recognized as the son, then Ishmael was cast out. It is Christ dwelling in us who sets us free. "Walk in the Spirit, and you shall not fulfill the lust of the flesh. Those who are Christ's have crucified the flesh with its passions and desires" (Galatians 5:16, 24).

Now at last God's way with Abraham was complete. We come to chapter 22, and it is to God's glory that here He could still test His servant. "It came to pass after these things that God tested Abraham." How many of us can stand being tested yet again, when all the lessons have already been learned?

What God now demanded of Abraham was nothing less than the outright sacrifice of his son. The Old Testament story emphasizes the emotional crisis this was for Abraham personally. "Take now your son, your only son Issac, whom you love, and go to the land of Moriah, and offer him there as a burnt offering."

But it is in the New Testament that we are shown the real costliness of this demand. Far more than mere human feelings were at issue. "By faith Abraham, when he was tested, offered up Isaac, and he who had received the promises offered up his only begotten son, of whom it was said, 'In Isaac your seed shall be called,' concluding that God was able to raise him up, even from the dead, from which he also received him in a figurative sense" (Hebrews 11:17–19). Isaac was the son God had promised, the hope of his posterity. That was the thing at stake—namely, God's matchless purpose of love. The son was not merely a personal matter to Abraham. If this heir of the promise died, upon whom hung the entire plan of God, then what remained?

Thus it was that this third test came to Abraham, not as an individual but as a vessel of the divine purpose. For all the fullness of promise was settled upon Isaac. To sacrifice him was to sacrifice the covenant word of God. The very witness to God in the nations turned upon this young man, and he was to be given up!

"Ishmael was *mine*, so to turn him out was reasonable; I respect that. But Isaac—he is not, in that sense, mine. He came by promise, entirely from God. I did not even ask for him; God *gave* him. Now He wants me to give him back! And He is not even taking him naturally by death; *I* must sacrifice him. In the first place I didn't want him, for I had Ishmael; so why did God give him? Having so wonderfully given him, why not leave him? But to give him and then to ask for him back? It is not reasonable!"

Once again Abraham must know God as *Father*. Isaac truly was from God. There was no problem there. The problem now was with Abraham's concern for Isaac. We must not become tied up possessively with God's gifts. Abraham had learned that God was Father in the birth of Isaac; he must learn that God is still Father after his birth. We often recognize it before Isaac comes, but when we look at Isaac— we cannot do without Isaac!

The question is, is it still God who occupies our vision, or Isaac? Before Isaac's birth, the two were one. Now they have become two, representing two claims upon our attention. We think, now that Isaac is come, that God's work is done and everything turns upon him. But God's promise is still with Himself, not with His gift.

Isaac can stand for many things. He represents many gifts of God's grace. Before God gives them, our hands are empty. Afterward they are full. Sometimes God reaches out His hand to take ours in fellowship. Then we need an empty hand to put into His. But when we have received His gifts and are nursing them to ourselves, our hands are full, and when God puts out His hand we have no empty hand for Him. We can dwell on His gifts at the neglect of Him. Often we forget that our experience is not for our lifelong use. Our source of life is God, not our experience. We hold onto the experience and forget God is Father. Let go of the gift and the experience, and hold onto God! Isaac can be done without, but God is eternal.

But as we have said, this matter of Isaac goes deeper. It is concerned with more than individual matters—with God's gift to us personally and with our personal experiences of Him. Isaac was intimately linked with God's will. In fact, Abraham might have been led to feel that Isaac in fact represented God's will and therefore must be held on to for *that* reason. But at the risk of seeming to press this matter excessively we must affirm that the will of God is not bound up with any *Isaac* but with *God Himself.*

It will help us if we compare together two chapters in the New Testament, Luke 22 and John 18, which helpfully illumine this passage. In the Garden of Gethsemane Jesus knelt and prayed, saying, "Father, if it is Your will, take this cup from Me; nevertheless not My will, but Yours, be done" (Luke 22:42). This request of His that the cup might pass from Him does not represent fear of the cross. We cannot doubt our Lord's courage. If martyrs have gladly died for Him through the ages, certainly their Lord did not fear crucifixion.

But there is a distinction here between what Jesus called the cup and the will. The cup was surely the work that God had sent him to do, and this included the cross. The will was something lying behind that, in the heart of God Himself. The cup in this passage is just one work—redemption. Jesus knew He had come for that work, even before He left heaven. Yet He had not become so bound to it that He could not let it go. There was an "if possible" in it, and of course there were real human reasons why some other alternative might be welcome, if God so willed. But for Him there was no "if possible" about God's will; *that* must be done, "possible" or not. Right up to the night before His crucifixion, Jesus never thought, "I must be crucified at all costs," but only, "I must do the will of Him who sent Me." The one is subsidiary and might possibly be changed; the other, the will of God, is something in God Himself, and must be done. Important— nay, vital—as the cross most certainly was, the Lord Jesus had not grasped it to Himself. All that mattered to Him was the Father's will, and the decision of how that will should be fulfilled remained in the Father's hands, not His.

So the cup represents the work, and the will represents God Himself. We are concerned with God Himself, not with the thing He wants us to do. With Christ the will of God was an ever-present thing, ever to be done. He was not even tied up to a single point in that will, such as the crucifixion. But when it was clear to Him that without any question the cross was in the will of God for Him, then with equal positiveness He said to Peter—and notice that these words follow the previous ones—"Shall I not drink the cup which My Father has given Me?" (John 18:11). Jesus puts first things first, the Father's will before the work which that will involves.

How perverse we are! Until Isaac comes we are like Abraham; we do not want him. But once Isaac has been given we cannot do without him, and we must hold onto him. First we oppose Isaac; then we possess him. That is what man is! And that is what Moriah deals with. It was Abraham's last test.

Do we love the work God has given us to do at the expense of the giver of it? Or is our fellowship with God the same, whether He gives or whether He withdraws our Isaac? Only as it is so can what Isaac represents be maintained upon the earth. Praise God, Abraham did not murmur at all. He did not even use the word "sacrifice." He said, "The lad and I will go yonder and worship, and we will come back to you" (Genesis 22:5). This experience really was worship to him.

Then it was that God could give Isaac back. The possessive bond was already broken. The attitude of Abraham's heart was, "I dare not think too much of Isaac. I don't know what God is going to do with him."

But out of this experience there came a further thing for Abraham; he discovered that God was not only the God of creation but also of resurrection. Hebrews 11:19 tells us that he concluded "that God was able to raise him up, even from the dead, from which he also received him in a figurative sense." In this also he knew God as Father, and for this too he was reckoned righteous. "Was not Abraham our father justified by works when he offered Isaac his son on the altar? Do you see that faith was working together with his works, and by works faith was made perfect? And the scripture was fulfilled which says, 'Abraham believed God, and it was accounted to him for righteousness.' And he was called the friend of God" (James 2:21–23). Everything that is really of value to us, even the work God gives us, and even our knowledge of God's will, must go through death to resurrection. In resurrection we know it to be something so miraculously of God that we can never again take it possessively into our hands. Resurrection puts it out of our reach. Isaac is born in my home, but he dwells in God's. He is not mine, I cannot hold him. God has become everything. This accords with the opening words of God's promise to Abraham there on the mount. "By Myself I have sworn, says the LORD" (22:16). There is nothing greater than that.

The fully developed promise that follows is very wonderful. "Because you have done this thing, and have not withheld your son, your only son—blessing I will bless you, and multiplying I will multiply your descendants as the stars of the heaven and as the sand which is on the seashore; and your descendants shall possess the gate of their enemies. In your seed all the nations of the earth shall be blessed, because you have obeyed My voice." Abraham's call was first for the land, second for the people of God, and now, third, for "all the nations of the earth."

Through deep experience Abraham has come to know God, not just as the giver of gifts but as the *Father*, the source of everything. It was this that qualified *him* to be the father of those who believe. It was this that fitted him to be God's vessel in the divine program of recovery.

Isaac:

the Son Given

9

The Wealth of the Child of God

THE SACRIFICE of Isaac is the believer's deepest lesson. It puts to us very straightly the question, Is our hope and expectation still in God, or is it in God *and* the Isaac we are holding on to? Or, worse still, is our hope in our Isaac only? After all, only God can fulfill His own purpose. When I was without Isaac, I looked to God. With Isaac, I still look to God just the same.

Abraham had come not only into the land but into the heart of God. He had become God's vessel, through whom God could do His work of recovery. This was no mere matter of justification by faith but of the *man* who was justified. God had secured the man He wanted.

Abraham's experience is God's standard in dealing with His people. Today God wants not only an Abraham but a corporate vessel. So Abraham's experience must be that of each individual, not only as such but also as a member of one body. For us all, His purpose is that we should together be Abraham's seed.

Ah, we may say, Abraham's experience is wonderful, only I am no Abraham. In Genesis 22 Abraham shines. After all these years I've never shone! Abraham is God's model vessel, certainly, but how can I ever arrive where Abraham did? God fulfilled His purpose in Abraham. Can He possibly do so in me?

Remember what we said at the beginning. God is not only the God of Abraham but also of Isaac and Jacob. This should serve to remind us at least that Abraham does not stand alone, complete and sufficient in himself as God's vessel for the fulfillment of His purpose. Isaac and Jacob were also needed along with him. Moreover, if we are to take our part in that purpose, we must know not only the God of Abraham but also the God of Isaac and of Jacob. We must have the experience of these two also, and as we look at their experience we shall find our questions begin to be answered. Abraham is the standard, it is true, but between him and the kingdom of Israel there are these other two. The corporate vessel is secured through the witness of all three. When God is the God of Abraham, of Isaac, and of Jacob, and when His people know Him as that, then the kingdom comes.

Abraham was the father *par excellence*. He had to learn to know God as originator, but the peculiarity of God's work upon him was that it made *him* original in more senses than one. He was a true forefather in that he was a pioneer. He was the first man in Scripture to forsake everything; to "cross over" to Canaan and so be designated a Hebrew; to have intimate fellowship with God as man to man; to beget an heir at one hundred years of age; to reject his own natural son in favor of God's miraculous gift; and then to sacrifice that gift at God's behest.

But if Abraham was the father, immediately we see Isaac as a figure of Christ the Son. No history so typifies Christ as does that of Isaac. Constituted the heir by divine promise, he was born not according to the flesh but according to the spirit (Galatians 4:29). Apart from Christ there was no other of whom this was said. Let us briefly recount some other ways in which Isaac may be a type of Christ. To Sarah, Isaac was Abraham's only true son, the beloved (Hebrews 11:17). Laid by his father on the altar, he was received back as from the dead to be to him the risen one. After Sarah herself died and her "age of grace" was past, Isaac's bride, a figure of the Church, was brought to him from a far country. Yet she came to him as the Church of God's will, not brought in from without but born from within, for Rebekah and Isaac were of one blood, one family, as are Christ and His own. Moreover, Isaac really did occupy his inheritance. Abraham at one point went down into Egypt and Jacob returned to Mesopotamia, but Isaac was born, lived, and died in Canaan. This is the Son who "is in heaven" (John 3:13), who never left His Father's bosom.

So in remarkable detail Isaac is a type of Christ. But leaving aside his typical significance, we must look now at the practical lessons to be learned from his experience. His is in fact the most ordinary experience in the Old Testament. He was a man seemingly without distinctive character, and in this respect is just the opposite of Abraham. Abraham did many things that no one else had done. Isaac did nothing that another had not already done.

Ishmael mocked Isaac—and Isaac said nothing. He took no initiative. He followed his father to Moriah and there allowed himself to be laid on the altar—without uttering a word. What his father did, he accepted. He merely asked one question; no more.

Even about his own marriage he had nothing to say. He knew nothing of the woman, and was not even consulted by his father about her choice. From the human standpoint everything he did was passive, negative. To us he is the son "doing nothing of himself" (John 5:19).

At sixty Isaac himself had two sons. Abraham had had to take action in respect of his children; he had had to cast out his eldest son. Isaac did nothing of the kind; nor was he asked to lay his son on the altar. Everything was difficult for Abraham; everything was straightforward for Isaac. He could not even sin with originality; his sin at Gerah was a replica of his father's! Three wells were dug by Abraham; Isaac simply reopened them. When Abimelech went to see Abraham, Abraham rebuked him for damage done to the wells. When he went to make a covenant with Isaac, Isaac only asked him why his servants had done such damage; he gave him no rebuke.

In his old age Isaac at last did have his own ideas about blessing his sons. He wanted to bless Esau. But God would not let him do something his father had not done; he too had to bless the younger son! In the end, even the tomb in which Isaac was laid was the one provided by his father.

In a sense Isaac is the complement of Abraham. Abraham embodies God's plan, God's standard. Isaac represents God's life, God's power. To see Abraham by himself, without the help of Isaac, is hard for us. Many see God's demands, and they cannot compass them, because they have not seen His provision. They see the standard, but not the life that satisfies that standard. Isaac gives us a picture of the life.

To Isaac Abraham gave all that he had (Genesis 24:36; 25:5). Isaac did not have to labor, to toil, to spend time in order to get it. All was bestowed upon him. Abraham attained, through long trials; Isaac inherited, in a single outright gift. Of all that he received, nothing was his own work. He did not even have to travel to reach Canaan as his father did; he was born there.

So much for his relationship with his father. When we look at his relationship with God we find the same thing. The promise to Isaac in Genesis 26:2–5 is exactly the same promise as is given to Abraham, and contains the words "I will perform the oath which I swore to Abraham your father." There was nothing new in it that was not promised to Abraham already. And its fulfillment was stated to be "because Abraham obeyed My voice and kept My charge, My commandments, My statutes, and My laws." Again, when the Lord appears to Isaac at Beersheba, He speaks of Himself as "the God of your father Abraham" and assures him that "I am with you. I will bless you and multiply your descendants for My servant Abraham's sake" (26:24). All was bestowed upon Isaac because he was Abraham's son.

This fact of bestowal and acceptance is the great characteristic of Isaac. The God of Isaac is God the giver. He is the God who comes out to us. We must know Him in this way as well as knowing Him as Father. If we only know Him as the God of Abraham there is no approach to Him. As the God of Isaac He comes to us and gives us everything in His Son. None can go forward and attain to God's purpose unless he knows how to receive in this way. Romans chapter 7 offers us a picture of the man who has not yet found the God of Isaac. He is forever under the law, and cries constantly: "To will is present with me, but how to perform what is good I do not find" (v. 18). He has not seen that everything is offered to him in Christ, nor how full that provision is. The secret is receiving, not doing. The way through is not by the exercise of the will but by the law of the Spirit of life in Christ Jesus (Romans 8:2). We know what the God of Abraham wants—we can't help knowing—but we don't know how to get there until we have found the God of Isaac. Victory, life, salvation—all is bestowed, not attained. When you are born into a wealthy home, it is very difficult to be poor! You are rich; you were *born* that way.

We never worked for our salvation, gradually scaling the heights until we attained to it. The Lord sought and saved us. Victory over sin is the same; it is received, not worked for. Oh, may we learn to praise God that He has provided for us such bounty in Christ!

Peter says that we "have escaped" from the corruption that is in the world (2 Peter 1:4). He does not say that we "are able to" escape, or that we "hope to" escape, but that *we have already done so*. This is the God of Isaac. What God has done, we receive and enjoy. We are not constantly waiting, hoping, anxiously seeking for it. We are born into the home; we have it all. Inheritance is ours.

Let us get quite clear what the life of the believer is. It is not "from here to there." It is "from there to here." It starts in God. As Paul says, it is the parents who lay up for the children and not the other way around (2 Corinthians 12:14).

Some of us force ourselves to do things we don't want to

do and to live a life we cannot in fact live, and think that in making this effort we are being Christians. That is very far removed from what Isaac was. The Christian life is lived when I receive the life of Christ within me as a gift, to live by that life. It is the nature of the life of Christ not to love the world but to be distinct from it, and to value prayer and the Word and communion with God. These are not things I do naturally; by nature I have to force myself to do them. But God has provided another nature, and He wants me to benefit from the provision He has made.

The only question Isaac asked was, "Where is the lamb?" The answer is full of meaning: "God will provide for Himself the lamb." That is the life of Isaac. We ask, and the answer is always the same: "God Himself will provide." So Abraham called the place of resurrection "Jehovah-jireh." Everything that is demanded, God Himself gives: that is the experience of Isaac. In Abraham God sets up a standard; in Isaac He shows us His storehouse. Strength, life, grace from God, all are ours to receive that we may measure up to the divine standard of a vessel for testimony.

We have looked at Abraham and Isaac; we must look for a moment at Isaac and Jacob, for Isaac lies between the two. In the comparisons just now before us, we have seen what God is giving *to* us. But we cannot stay there; we must also ask what it is that God is securing *in* us. We know that Christ is all. But in us there is a rival to Christ, namely, our own strength of nature. That too must find its answer, and when we have dealt with Isaac, that answer will be the theme of our final chapters.

Isaac received everything, and by his very passivity sets forth God's bountiful grace. Jacob lost everything, and in his trials exemplifies the rigors of God's chastening hand. In Isaac God ministers to us the triumphant resurrection life of Christ. In Jacob we see the other side of the coin; for God is compelled, for Christ's sake, to apply to us the discipline of the Spirit. The life of nature in us is being reduced progressively to its zero, that Christ may be fully displayed. God's work in Jacob will in fact be to make room for the God of Isaac.

10

The Status of an Heir

THE DISTINCTIVE feature of true Christianity is that it compels people to receive. The letter to the Galatians draws a close parallel between ourselves and Isaac, and shows that we are people who receive just as he did. We are heirs (3:29; 4:7). We partake of the promises (3:22; 4:28). There is an inheritance in view, and we enter into that inheritance (3:18; 4:30 ff.). In all these things we are at the receiving end.

Ishmael was born into slavery. His mother was a bond-woman and he shared her status. Slavery was his inheritance. But Isaac, because of the status of his mother, was born to freedom. In New Testament terms Sarah represents grace, just as Hagar represents law (4:24 ff.). Grace means that salvation is a free gift of God, for which we do not work. He does it all.

In Paul's letter to the Romans he makes it clear that the sinner depends on grace for his salvation. In these chapters of Galatians he shows that the believer depends equally upon grace for his continuation in the Christian life. We never did anything, or gave God anything, for our salvation. Now we are to go on in the same way, not making even faith something that we do but looking trustfully to His grace and continuing to receive. For Christ has prepared for us everything.

There are two sides to Christ's work, expressed in two simple statements. First, you and I are in Christ. Second, Christ is in you and in me. Every fruit of our union with Christ is governed by these two statements of what God has done. The Lord Jesus Himself puts this in a concise sentence which says: "Abide in Me, and I in you" (John 15:4)

By virtue of our position in Christ we benefit from all the accomplished facts of His history: His life on earth, His death and resurrection, and His session at God's right hand. All His work becomes ours—all that He has already done and that is covered by the statement, "It is finished." By virtue of the further fact that Christ is in us, we become partakers of His life. All His power, all that He can do now, all that He is today, becomes ours. Both these aspects of our union with Him are included in our inheritance; if we want to enter into all our inheritance then we must see them both. If we only know that we are in Christ, we are passive and weak. If we only know that Christ is in us, life is uphill and something is missing. Neither is sufficient alone. Both are gifts already given to us to provide for our life, our future, our standing before God, our practical holiness—everything.

God begins by giving us a new position so that we have a new start. He does this by placing us in Christ. If I am down at the bottom of a horrible pit, then I continue there with no way of getting out of it, until God lifts me out and puts me upon a rock. That is what He has done for us in Christ.

By placing us in Him He has settled all our past, just as by placing the life of Christ within us He has given us all we need for the present and for the entire future. The two sides are necessary to deliver us out of our agonized striving to attain and into that place of rest, where all is from God.

How we need that new start in Christ! We are sinners in God's sight and we need deliverance and a new standing before God. We shall never have it in ourselves.

I belong to the race of Adam, and I have only Adam in me. Not only is my conduct bad but *I* am bad. The man himself is wrong and not merely his actions.

As young Christians we take a long time to learn this. Only after bitter experience does it dawn on us that it is no mere question of dropped goods but of the faultiness of the bag containing them. If we find one thing after another dropping out of our pockets, we eventually give up putting them back in there. We feel around instead to see if perchance the pocket has a hole in it! It is the unfailing recurrence of our sins of hasty speech, quick temper, avid self-seeking and so on, that—even when we know God's forgiveness—exposes the fact that the trouble is within ourselves.

The apostle Paul makes this clear in the first section of Romans where, down to the beginning of chapter 5, he shows us how man's conduct is wrong, and how the cure for this is God's forgiveness through the precious blood of Christ. Then in the second section, down to chapter 8, he shows us how the man *himself* is wrong and must be dealt with. What is the remedy here? It is one thing only: for that man *himself* to die.

God does not say "the soul that sins must get his sins cleansed"; He says "the soul that sins must die." "He who has died," says Paul, "has been freed [acquitted] from sin" (Romans 6:7). There is no other remedy. In the sight of God we must die.

But what sort of salvation would be ours if we were to end there? There is the need for a resurrection to new life, and a new start. We must not only die in God's eyes, we must rise again. But surely, too, there must be a new position. I must not only *live* but I must live *for God*; and He is in heaven, so I must *ascend* there. Thus there must be a death, a resurrection and an ascension before the trouble I have inherited from Adam is reversed.

How can this possibly be? How can I die, and be raised, and ascend to where God is? The simple answer is that I cannot. Man may seek this kind of death, but he can never attain it. He may seek resurrection, and all he achieves is a grave. He may seek heaven, but he finds himself earthbound. To escape from the inheritance of Adam and from sin's reign is an insuperable problem.

There is indeed only one solution, and this is clearly stated in 1 Corinthians 1:30. The Chinese version of the statement is: "That you are in Christ Jesus, is of God."* This is a most important affirmation. It is God's work that has placed me in Christ Jesus. It is nothing that I have done or could ever do. And everything for my salvation stems from the fact that God has done it.

You have seen this illustration before, but I will repeat it. I have a bus ticket here, and I put it into the pages of this book. Now I put the book into the fire and burn it. What happens to the ticket? Or I throw the book into the river.

---

* The NIV reads: "It is because of him [God] that you are in Christ Jesus." And the NASB reads: "But by His doing you are in Christ Jesus."

What about the ticket? Or again, I make the book up into a parcel, and take it to the post office and mail it to Europe. Where is the ticket now? You can answer each question with absolute assurance; and yet it is a fact that once it was in the book, I did nothing more with the ticket as such. I did not send the ticket to Europe, I sent the book. Because the ticket is in the book, where the book goes the ticket must go. It has a part in everything that happens to the book. When I tell you what has happened to the book, you do not have to stop and puzzle over what has happened to the item that is included in the book.

We have been placed *into Christ*. When Christ was put to death we *died* in Him, because we *are* in Him (Romans 6:6). Moreover, the work of God did not stop there, for the Lord Jesus rose and ascended to the Father's right hand. But because we *are* in Christ Jesus, we also were *made alive* with Him, and *raised*, and *seated* with Him in the heavenly places (Ephesians 2:5 ff.). We have a new standing in the presence of God, and it is not something to which we attained but something which is ours because we are *in Christ*. These facts, which are historically true of Him, become real also in our experience.

It is important to realize that Scripture makes our death, resurrection and ascension to be "given" historic facts in Christ. The fact that our old man was crucified with Him is something we know (Romans 6:6). Unless we have cause to reckon ourselves not to be "in Christ," we cannot say that these facts are untrue. They follow logically from what God has done in the initial step of our salvation.

I cannot sufficiently emphasize that this is the first element in our inheritance in Christ. Our death in Christ Jesus, and the freedom from sin which goes with that death, are not doctrine but inheritance. They are not things that I have to do but gifts that I have *received*. However hard I try, I shall only prove to myself that by striving it does not work. But if I see that *God* has worked, and that the "old man" who has been such a problem *was crucified* long ago, then I shall know what it is to walk in newness of life.

Here I must share with you my own experience. Thirteen years ago I came to the point where I knew that there was a lack somewhere in my life. Sin was defeating me, and I saw that something was fundamentally wrong. I asked God to show me what was the meaning of the expression, "I have been crucified with Christ." For some months I prayed earnestly and read the Scriptures, seeking light. It became increasingly clear to me that, when speaking to us on this subject, God nowhere says, "You must be," but always "You have been." Yet in view of my constant failures this just did not seem possible, unless I was to be dishonest with myself. I almost turned to the conclusion that only dishonest people could make such statements.

Then one morning I came in my reading to 1 Corinthians 1:30. "You are in Christ Jesus," it said. I looked at it again. "That you are in Christ Jesus, is God's doing!" It was amazing! Then if Christ died—and that is a certain fact—and if God put me into *Him*, then I must have died too. All at once I *saw*. I cannot tell you what a wonderful discovery that was.

The trouble with us today is that we think crucifixion with Christ is an experience we have somehow to attain. It is not. It is something *God* has done, and we have only to receive it. The whole difference lies here: Is the cross a doctrine to be grasped and then applied? Or is it a revelation which God flashes upon my heart? It is quite possible, as I have proved, to know and preach the doctrine of the cross without seeing the wonderful fact.

All God has done He has done first of all to Christ, and only then to us because we are *in* Christ. God does nothing directly upon us. Apart from and outside of Christ, God has no work of grace. Here is the preciousness of 1 Corinthians 1:30. God has not only given us Christ but Christ's *experience*; not only what He can do but what He has *already* done. From His death onward, all that He has is ours! This is the divine provision that Isaac illustrates to us.

But we must not stop there. We have seen the fact of Christ, of all that He has already done in the past which we now have in Him, and which settled our own past because we are in Christ. But the other side of the coin is this: that Christ is in us not for the past but for today and for all the *future*! His life is given to us, so that now He, exalted in heaven, is our life-power. I, in Him, have received His finished work. He, in me, gives me His power.

How can we be victorious, righteous, holy? First we must understand clearly that God has not constituted Christ our example to be copied. He is not giving us His strength to help us imitate Christ. He has not even planted Christ within us to help us to be Christlike. Galatians 2:20 is not our standard for record-breaking endeavor. It is not a high aim to be aspired to through long seeking and patient progress. No, it is not God's aim at all, but God's *method*. When Paul says "It is no longer I who live, but Christ lives in me," he is showing us how only Christ satisfies God's heart. This is the life that gives God satisfaction in the believer, and there is no substitute. "No longer I, but Christ," means Christ *instead of* me. When Paul uses these words he is not claiming to have attained something his readers have not yet reached to. He is defining the Christian life. The Christian life is the Christ life. *Christ* in me has become my life, and is living my life instead of me. It is not even that *I trust Him* as a separate, sufficient act. No, God gives Him to be my life.

Moreover, in the new life there is a law—the law that determines what that life is like in expression. It is not just that a *life* is present in me, for if this were all, I would then have to hold tightly onto it. No, there is a law of that life (Romans 8:2) and that law looks after itself.

When we put a book on a table, we do not always need carefully and precisely to place it right down on the table's surface. We can let it go, just as we can drop a piece of paper into a wastepaper basket. The law of gravity is working, and it insures that the book will fall into place. Without the law of gravity we would have to be more careful, or it might go up instead of down. But the law takes care of it, and we do not have to. Just so, *we* do not need to look after the law of life in Christ Jesus; the law will look after us!

Often we find something in the Christian life difficult, and so we turn to God for help. Really, that is wrong. We are trying to use the life instead of letting the life use us. Let go, and the law will operate, and the life itself will work. Say to God, "I cannot do it, but *Your* life in me can and will. I am putting my trust in You." There is not even the need—indeed, there is seldom the time—consciously to exert faith in this matter. There is a law, and a law must always work; we have only to rest in it. Like Isaac, we have everything done for us by the Father.

It is just here that the second half of 1 Corinthians 1:30 is so splendid. "Christ Jesus . . . became for us wisdom from God—and righteousness and sanctification and redemption." This means that my righteousness and yours is not a quality or a virtue; indeed it is not a thing at all—but a living person. My holiness is not a condition of life but a person. My redemption is not a hope but Christ in me, the hope of glory. Yes, Christ in me, and Christ in you—this is all we need.

The daily life of the Christian is summed up in the word "receive." Every challenging thing that God demands of me—long-suffering, meekness, humility, goodness, holiness, joy—is not something I *am*, or something I *do*, or some virtue I acquire or *attain* to. It is Christ in me. Each is the manifestation of *Him*. Let Him be revealed, naturally and spontaneously, and that is enough.

"He became for us. . . ." If it was written that He justifies, sanctifies, redeems, we could understand. But it does not say that He *does* these things. It uses abstract nouns: He *is* these things. Christ in us meets every demand of God, and every demand of the circumstances around us.

It is not in us to be humble, nor shall we find it helps to trust in the power of Christ to make us humble. Christ is humble, naturally—that is, by His very nature—and He is made our humility, for Christ is our all. Even faith and trust and obedience, if we regard them as virtues by which we attain, will prove ineffective. It is not that I trust His Word, therefore I can be long-suffering. It is that Christ is long-suffering, and, praise God, Christ is in *me*! Once again, this is Isaac—natural, simple, spontaneous, trusting implicitly and without question—because the Father has made absolutely sufficient provision.

11

The New Life Indwelling

I.T IS only through knowing God first as the God of Isaac that we can move on to know him as the God of Jacob. Unless we know our inheritance as something already secured and settled in Christ and given to us by God, we have no foundation for going on. To be brought under the discipline of the Spirit without first knowing that assurance of a work of God already done in Christ would be a terrible thing.

At the risk of laboring the point, let me say again: all that Christ has done, and all that we have in Him, *is already ours*. As children of God we are already in Christ; we are one with Him. We don't hope to be; it is already done. The only question is, do we really believe God's Word when we read it?

We have been crucified and buried and raised and seated together with Christ. If His death is past, so is ours. No man can say that Christ's death is future; then how can ours be? Ours is one hundred percent as complete and finished as

His; not ninety-nine percent! Not all the sin and weakness in the world can alter that fact; sin is another question entirely.

Before we see this, we long to die in order to escape from sinning. When, however, we see that we have already died in Christ, our outlook on both sin and death is completely changed. It is not prayerful people but praising ones who reach the way of holiness—those who see, and who seeing believe, and who believing praise.

Many of us read Romans 6:11: "Likewise you also, reckon yourselves to be dead to sin, but alive to God in Christ Jesus our Lord." Oh! we exclaim, I have tried that. I have tried to reckon myself dead to sin, but I always find I have sinned before I have had time to get the reckoning done!

But what is reckoning? Here is a five-dollar bill in my wallet. I reckon I have five dollars, for the simple reason that I have it here. What use would be reckoning if I didn't have it? Reckoning means bookkeeping—keeping accounts. And common sense tells us that accounts must bear a direct relation to the cash in the till.

God commands us to reckon ourselves dead because we *are* dead, and for no other reason. "Our old man was crucified with Him" (6:6), and we know this. Therefore we are told to count upon it. The *fact* of the death comes before our reckoning on it, not the other way around. That is the difference between victory and defeat. The money is in my wallet, whether I reckon it is there or not; and I am dead with Christ, whether I reckon upon the fact or not. On the cross of Christ, God included me in Him, and so I have been crucified.

Let me repeat that. It is not that I identify myself with

Christ; it is that God has included me in Him. He has already done it. This is something that can come to us with a flash of new understanding. Just as once God opened our eyes to see our sins laid *upon* Christ, so again He must open our eyes to see our own selves *in* Christ. And this is something He delights to do. Suddenly we see with a flash of insight that all that Christ has already done has become *ours*. This union with Christ in death disposes of our whole unhappy past.

But this negative value to us of the *finished work* of Christ in respect of the old way of life is matched by a positive value to us of His *living person* in respect of the new. God comes with this further revelation to my heart, that Christ *is in me*. Christ is my life, fighting for me, triumphing on my behalf, doing what He wants to do in me, and *doing it now.*

It is not that I have strength through Him to seek humility, meekness, holiness. He is all that in me; for He is my life. The Christian has not a lot of odds and ends of virtues; indeed, he has *no* virtues; he just has Christ. The question is again, do we believe God's Word? Do we believe 1 Corinthians 1:30?

Oh yes, we know we *should* have victory, so when we meet with a temptation we take great care, and we watch, and we pray. We feel it is our duty to fight against that thing and to reject it, so we make up our minds not to yield, exerting our wills to the utmost. But *that* is not our victory. *Christ* is our victory. We do not need will power and determination to resist the tempter. We look to Him who is our life. "Lord, this is Your affair; I count on You. The victory is Yours, and You, not I, shall have the credit." So often we gain a kind of victory and everyone knows about it! We achieved it ourselves; but communion with our Lord is broken and there is no peace.

Many of us live in constant fear of temptation. We know just how much we can stand, but alas, we have not discovered how much *Christ* can stand. "I can stand temptation up to a point, but beyond that point, I am done for." If two children cry, the mother can stand it, but if more than two cry together, under she goes. Yet it is not really a matter of whether two children cry, or three. It is all a question of whether I am getting the victory or *Christ*. If it is I, then I can stand two only. If Christ, it won't matter if twenty cry at once! To be carried through by Christ is to be left wondering afterward how it happened!

This, too, is a matter that God delights to bring to us with a new flash of understanding. Suddenly one day we see that *Christ is our life* (Colossians 3:4). That day everything is changed.

There is a day when we see ourselves in Christ. After that, nothing can make us see ourselves outside of Him. It alters everything. Then also there is a day when we see that Christ within us is our *life*. That too alters our whole outlook. They may be different days with an interval between, or both may come together. But we must have both; and when we do, then we begin to know Christ's fullness, and to marvel that we have been so stupid hitherto as to remain poor in God's storehouse. Ours is the God of Isaac. We are entering into God's inheritance.

It is now that we can begin to look at the difference between the God of Isaac and the God of Jacob. Isaac, as we have said, speaks to us of God's impartation to us of Christ, whereas Jacob illustrates our disciplinary schooling by the

Holy Spirit. Isaac reminds us of God's gifts made over to us absolutely, a reminder that gives us wonderful confidence and assurance. Jacob, on the other hand, draws our attention to the Spirit's inward working upon us to form Christ within, a working whose costliness draws forth rather our fear and trembling. Isaac is able to witness to victory in Christ. Jacob causes us to know our own extreme weakness and uselessness. In Isaac we boldly proclaim that sin is beneath our feet; yet in Jacob we tremblingly confess that as long as we live we may fall again. Isaac assures us that Christ's fullness is ours, so that we may confidently praise Him. Jacob recalls our attention from Christ to the Christian, to our deficient and inadequate selves.

The contrasts we have adduced above represent two experiences that run parallel throughout Scripture and are integral to our Christian life. The trouble is that we are apt to give our attention to one of the two only. There are, on the one hand, some very strong, almost extreme words in Scripture. "God . . . always leads us in triumph." Sin shall not have dominion over you." "To me to live is Christ." "I can do all things through Christ." They are bold, strong, almost boastful affirmations. Yet the same people who say these things must also say: "I was with you in weakness, and in fear, and in much trembling." "I am chief of sinners." (Note there the present tense in the Greek.) "We have no hope in ourselves." "The blood of Jesus His Son cleanses us from all sin." "If we say that we have no sin, we deceive ourselves." "We also are weak in Him." "When I am weak, then am I strong." "Most gladly therefore will I rather glory in my weaknesses."

So we see another kind of Christian, utterly weak, sinful,

trembling. We see another kind of Christian life, altogether lacking in self-confidence. These two together, Isaac with his confidence in Christ and Jacob with his self-knowledge, are the life of the Christian.

It is because we only see one side of this that there are so many divergencies among those who preach the victorious life. We must know Christ's fullness, but we must also know our own corruption. These are things we must see, and these are what the God of Jacob shows us through the schooling of the Spirit, until we reach the place where we really know ourselves. In too many of us there is a departmental knowledge of God. We know the fatherhood of God, but not the positiveness of Christ. Or we know this too, but lack the brokenness of the Spirit. Some know the God of Jacob without knowing the God of Isaac; they see their own weakness, but do not know Christ's strength. No wonder they feel depressed about it! If we want a full knowledge of God we must know Him in all of these three ways, and even then we shall find that we are constantly making further progress!

Jacob:

The Real Transformation

12

Precious Stones

THE LESSONS taught to us from the life of Jacob concern the Holy Spirit's discipline of the Christian. It is this that makes room in our lives for Christ to reveal Himself. This discipline is concerned not with our old man and his sinfulness but with our natural strength, the strength of *self*. Before we are saved they are as one, and we cannot distinguish between them; but in the Christian they are clearly distinguished in Scripture.

At his creation in the Garden of Eden, Adam had by nature a distinct self-conscious personality, but he had no sin, no "old man." He possessed free will, which made it possible for him to act on his own account, so that self was already there—but not sin.

Natural strength is what we receive from the hand of God as Creator. Spiritual strength is what we receive from God in grace. At our birth we receive wisdom, skill, intellect, eloquence, feelings, consciousness, and all these go to make up our personality as man—apart from sin. But after Adam's fall, he changed. Sin had come in and taken control of him. Now he was not only a natural man, the "old man" also was there in him; he was under the dominion of sin, loving to sin. Before he sinned, Adam was a *natural* man. After he sinned, he was the *old* man.

We must be cautious about drawing parallels between ourselves and the Lord Jesus in His incarnation, but we can say with assurance that Jesus had no old man, because He was free from sin. Nevertheless He had a self; He possessed natural strength. Yet not once, in the smallest degree, did He ever abuse it. That is the difference. It is not that He did not possess personality and individualism—everyone must have these—but that He did not choose to live by Himself. "I can of Myself do nothing" (John 5:30). This was His estimate of the worthlessness of natural human effort apart from God. We can understand, therefore, why He went on to say of our spiritual fruitfulness: "Without Me you can do nothing" (15:5).

Unlike Him, we ourselves possess an old man, sold under sin. It is he that must be put out of the way, and as we saw, God has already done this on the cross in Christ. But that is only the beginning of God's problem with us, for there is still our natural man to be dealt with. We not only sin in the sight of God, we do many things with the best intention of pleasing God that are mistimed and misdirected and fail altogether to satisfy Him. Take the man who is always indiscriminately broadcasting all he knows about spiritual things. That is not the old man but the *natural* man at work. To speak of spiritual things is not sin, but the natural man is doing it out of his own zeal and not because the Lord wants it.

The natural life is just that, doing what we want and not what God wants. We may do many quite good things, building quite an impressive edifice on the foundation that is Jesus Christ. Nevertheless, God calls them wood, hay, and straw (1 Corinthians 3:12). Such materials are not refuse but represent things done by man. True, the man is doing God's work of building; yet the work is judged. It is not a question of whether the workmanship is good or bad, but of who is doing the work.

The difference between the natural man and the old man is a basic one. God has given us His Son. When we enter into Him and He into us, what happens? One day we receive Him as our Savior and Lord, and quickly discover that our old man was dealt with once and for all in His cross (Romans 6:6). God made no effort to patch him up or improve him, but crucified him outright in Christ, finishing him for good. Therein the question of sin was settled. To know this is of the greatest importance. In God's eyes the old man had to die. Then our eyes are opened and the truth dawns on us that he is already dead in Christ; and that Christ Himself is our new life, indwelling, empowering, becoming to us everything. This is a tremendous discovery.

But along with this new life indwelling, there remains within us the natural man, the good, honest, worthy human nature that wants to please God. It is this that God encounters in Jacob.

God's dealings with Jacob as a man concern the question of his fulfilling the divine will. Jacob was interested in this above all, not in sinning. He knew that God had said of himself and his brother, "the older shall serve the younger" (Genesis 25:23). Accordingly he set himself to achieve this.

He used human means to reach the divine end, for he was set on spiritual things and on fulfilling God's will. Only he made the fundamental mistake of setting about it in his own way.

God not only hates man's sin, He has no room for the natural man. Not merely did our Lord Jesus never sin, He never depended upon Himself to do good—indeed to do anything at all. God's dealings with our natural man are designed to bring us to the place that Christ Himself chose to take. By nature we are so strong, so able to think and plan and do, and God must bring us to the place of weakness, the place where we cannot think or plan or do things apart from Him.

As we have just said, nothing is ever done to the old man; he died in Christ. Something, however, is done to the natural man. He is not patched up, it is true; he is weakened. He is progressively incapacitated. Step by step the Spirit weakens our natural life until at length, by a last drastic divine touch, we are as *dead* before Him. But for what? To show us what? To lead us where?

We saw that "I in Christ" leads to "Christ in me," the outward fact leading to an inward fact, both of them accomplished acts of God. In the same way, the progressive discipline of the Spirit through outward circumstances leads to a formation of Christ within us by the Spirit (Galatians 4:19) so that we live a life that is in a new sense derived from Him.

In the figure of Isaac we have Christ imparted to us so that, in the words of Galatians 2:20, it is "no longer I who live, but Christ lives in me." In the figure of Jacob we have Christ being *wrought* in us, so that "the life which I now live in the flesh I live by faith in the Son of God." It is the Holy

Spirit's work to form Christ in us in this latter way. God deals with the natural man that Christ may be inwrought in us, so that we manifest the fruit of the Spirit (5:22).

Hebrews 12:5–11 speaks of the loving chastening of the Lord. God, who is the Father of our spirits, deals with us as sons; and He does so to our profit, that we may be partakers of His holiness. This is clearly different from 1 Corinthians 1:30, where it is made plain that Christ *is* holiness. Here in Hebrews 12, through trial and suffering, I come to be a *partaker* of His holiness. This is something constructive. Something is being wrought in me. Grievous suffering is yielding peaceable fruit—fruit that is produced by the Spirit of God, effortlessly.

What do I mean by that? Let us take the example we have used already. Our human nature delights to expose its spiritual experiences. We prattle on about what the Lord has taught us of deliverance from sin (I am not here referring to "witness," that is a different matter) and then the thing we claimed had been finally dealt with in us happens again! We are shattered. And this recurs—until spontaneously we learn not to prattle any more. We do not *decide* not to talk; we just *don't* talk. We have learned through suffering.

Here, in this small lesson, we have a tiny particle of what is meant by the term "Christ inwrought." In this small degree of self-restraint the character of Christ has become in practice ours. The Spirit is developing in us a new character.

The items listed in Galatians 5:22–23 under the heading of "the fruit of the Spirit" are not virtues that the Spirit gives us; they are the natural, spontaneous fruit of the new character. The good tree is bearing good fruit, just as when a peach and a pear tree are planted side by side in the same kind of soil and given the same care and water and nourishment and sunshine, but each of them bears its own distinctive fruit. These outward things are absorbed by each, and by each they are changed into their own fruit. Just so, the sunshine of Christ's own life is transmuted in us into something that is recognizably our own.

What God wants today is first that we should know Christ as our *life*, and in addition, that the Spirit should work Christ into us, to become our *characters*. Few enough of us know what is meant by the impartation of Christ. Fewer still, alas, know the formation of Christ by the Spirit. Yet this is the whole object of God's dealing with us by chastening.

When we meet some aged saint who has gone through long years of discipline and perhaps suffering under the hand of God, we encounter a depth of spiritual measure, a Christ-likeness, which displays how really and deeply Christ has been wrought into them. (This is something the young lack, for of course such formation takes time.) Not only their life but the warp and woof of their *character* becomes Christ. It is, we may say, the Spirit's manufacture.

Some of us are naturally so capable, able to do anything. Others of us are impetuous, ready at once to act for God, impatient of delay. Peter was one such. God did not improve him but touched and weakened him, and then worked Christ into him. So, later on, we encounter in Peter not only a new life but a new *man*. Paul, too, was one who had had Christ wrought into him through the testings of time. "I have *learned*," says he, "in whatever state I am, to be content" (Philippians 4:11), and the context refers to physical want. Through such experience, which took time, there was a progressive but a quite definite change in his character.

And this is what we ourselves need: not only exchanged lives, where it is no longer I but Christ, but *changed* lives. Of course, we cannot have the second without the first, but God does indeed want the second; He does want a real transformation in us.

There was a real transformation in Paul, not just a doctrinal one. In 1 Corinthians 7 there are some verses where Paul speaks for himself, expressing a purely personal opinion. "But this I say by way of permission, not of commandment" (7:6). "But to the rest say I, not the Lord" (7:12). Who dares to speak like that? Yet God puts it into His Word. "But I give judgment as one whom the Lord in His mercy has made trustworthy" (7:25). There has been the formation of Christ in him, and what such a one says is valuable in the sight of God, *even though it be his own words*. Paul was a vessel for God's words, for he could also say, "I command, yet not I but the Lord" (7:10); but in these other instances he speaks on the ground of God's dealing with him and his oneness of heart with God, and thus God can confirm it. Only one who has known the formation of the Spirit can say, as Paul does, "Imitate me, just as I also imitate Christ" (1 Corinthians 11:1). If another man said this we would regard him as dangerously proud, but we are forced to acknowledge the power of God in those in whom the Spirit has wrought His formative work.

And this formative work is basic to Christianity. The command of Jesus in Matthew 28:19 is: "Go therefore and make disciples of all the nations." The believer receives salvation, but this is not enough, this is not the end. The disciple *learns*, and his life is worked upon by training and discipline. This is the ministry of the Holy Spirit.

This matter of the quality of life is expressed in figurative language at the beginning, in the middle, and at the end of the Bible. In Genesis 2:12 we read, "The gold of that land is good. Bdellium and the onyx stone are there." In 1 Corinthians 3:12 Paul tells us, "If anyone builds on this foundation with gold, silver, precious stones, wood, hay, straw, each one's work will become clear; for the Day will declare it, because it will be revealed by fire." And in Revelation 21:19–21 we read that "the foundations of the wall of the city were adorned with all kinds of precious stones; . . . and the twelve gates were twelve pearls; . . . and the street of the city was pure gold, like transparent glass."

God's purpose for mankind is not just gold but *precious stones*. "Gold" surely represents that which is of God, which proceeds from the Father. "Silver" stands for the redemption that is in Christ, His free gift of grace. "Precious stones"are the work of the Spirit. Stones are not elements, they are compounds. They are formed through fire, then cut. This is a figure of the Spirit's discipline; through much suffering, difficulty, sorrow—through stress of circumstances—we are made into gem stones. In the New Jerusalem there is no mention of silver at all; all has become precious stones.

God is looking for a vessel for the meeting of His need and the carrying out of His wondrous purpose. Such a vessel must know the God of Abraham, that all is from Him alone—gold. It must know the God of Isaac, that all is His gift in Christ—silver. It must know too the God of Jacob, the Spirit's dealing with the natural man that works Christ into the being—*precious stones*.

13

His Own Medicine

WHEN we begin to look at Jacob the man, we discover how strikingly his story is like our own. Before God has begun to deal with us we are inclined to take a rather superior attitude to Jacob, and judge him as self-willed and irresponsible. But when we begin to recognize the flesh in ourselves and our own weakness and sinfulness and self-will, then it is that we see Jacob in ourselves. And when we come to the last seventeen years of his life, and watch his words and his whole demeanor, we must praise God's grace in the man. It is hard to find anyone in the Old Testament with an end like his. It can move us to tears to see how wondrously God has worked in him and how grace has led him to a place of usefulness. A seemingly hopeless man has been made into a most useful vessel for God's purpose.

Yet the whole of this fruitfulness in Jacob was the result of God's discipline of him. God touched his natural strength, and as a result he became in due course a vessel for noble use. It is as the Spirit disciplines us that He works Christ into us; they are not two separate works. The life of Christ is wrought into the character of the disciple, and fruit is born naturally, spontaneously. So we have much to learn from Jacob.

We can recognize four stages in Jacob's life. First, the man Jacob as he was (Genesis 25–27). Second, his testing and discipline through circumstances (28–31). Third, the dislocation of his natural life (32–36). Fourth, the "peaceable fruit" (37–50).

We begin by looking at the character of Jacob the man. By natural instinct Jacob was a fighter from birth (Genesis 25:22–26). How different he was from Isaac! Isaac did nothing; he accepted and received everything. Jacob from beginning to end is a schemer—clever, wily, confident that he can do anything. How is God going to bring such a man to the place of being a vessel for His purpose?

It was not just that what he *did* was wrong; he himself, from before his birth, was a man unsuitable to God by *nature*. Oh yes, he desired the will of God. He wanted Esau to hold back and allow him, Jacob, to be the oldest; and when that did not happen he used every device, every stratagem to make good the disadvantage. That was Jacob! Of what use to God was such a man?

We cannot give a rational answer to that question. Only the grace of God can account for His choice of this one. "For the children not yet being born, nor having done any good or evil, that the purpose of God according to election might stand, not of works, but of Him who calls, it was said to [Rebekah], 'The older shall serve the younger.' As it is written, 'Jacob I have loved, but Esau I have hated'" (Romans 9:11–13). The election of God is the only explanation; there is no other. God wanted to choose a man. We must believe in the choice of God. If He has begun a good work in us He will not leave it half done. He is the first *and* the last. The work He has started to do in us He will finish. If we trust to the election of God we can *rest* in Him. If you are inclined to say "I am so difficult for God to deal with," then put your trust in Jacob's God. Jacob did not choose God; first, God chose Jacob. Before his birth He chose him, and the same is true of us. Recognize God's elective grace, and we shall be freed from anxiety.

It was the will of God that Jacob should rule. Jacob had discovered that. He learned of God's plan and recognized its true importance, and that it involved him and not his brother. He saw God's election and God's purpose, but he wanted to make sure of it for himself. So in their youth, when Esau returned one day from hunting, Jacob bargained with him for his birthright. "Let me be the older, and you shall be the younger," he declared (Genesis 25:29–34). His motive was right, but he used his own wits to get what God fully intended to give him.

Then, in chapter 27, Jacob cheated his father in order to secure his father's blessing. We can, of course, see Jacob's problem. Isaac had sent Esau to hunt, with a view to giving *him* his blessing. If that happened, and Esau received the blessing of the firstborn, then what about God's promise? Jacob had seen the design behind that promise, and so he saw the danger too. He must somehow contrive that God's will should be done. From his point of view he was quite right, but his was the reasoning of the natural man. Each thing Jacob did, we find, was designed to accomplish God's will. He showed, however, that he could not wait for God's time and look to God to do it but must himself devise measures to bring about what it appeared as though God could not do.

Our natural man uses human strength and ingenuity to compass the will of God. If God's throne seems in danger of falling, out goes our hand to steady it. "Something must be done!" we exclaim. That is Jacob, the able, scheming, clever, natural man. But the result of his efforts was only that Esau felt himself cheated and determined to kill him, and Jacob had to leave home.

Not only does man's uncleanness render him unfit, and therefore powerless, to do God's will; man's very best is equally powerless. No matter how perfect the heart's intentions may be, if it is man using his natural strength to do it, the result is failure. Jacob had not learned to know and quietly to wait for the God who says, "I will work, and who will reverse it?" (Isaiah 43:13). He was God's choice; God wanted him, but he knew neither God nor himself. The blessing he attained by cheating he failed truly to realize. All he received was God's discipline. Clever people get a lot of that!

Through discipline God gave him the blessing he had cheated to obtain. Already at Bethel, before he had even left the land, his life of discipline began (Genesis 28:10–22). God spoke to him in a dream. He could not speak to Jacob directly while he was trusting in his own plans.

But now, look what God at Bethel says to Jacob! "I am the Lord God of Abraham your father and the God of Isaac; the land on which you lie I will give to you and your descendants. Also your descendants shall be as the dust of the earth; you shall spread abroad to the west and the east, to the north and the south; and in you and in your seed all the families of the earth shall be blessed" (28:13–14). It would not surprise us if God had said these words at the end of Jacob's life, but here they are at the very outset! The whole blessing is presented to him, even while he is still his natural, contriving, crafty self. How is this possible? Surely only because God knew *Himself.* He had great confidence in what He Himself would do. He knew that this Jacob, so committed to Him, could not escape His hands, and sooner or later would become His vessel for noble use. "I will give it," God said. There was nothing for Jacob to do. How wonderful that God is a God of such confidence! He knows He can carry out his own plans.

We might well think such a downright statement of intention rather risky when dealing with a man like Jacob. But the end was already certain; God's plans always are. For God's expectation is in Himself, never in us. Oh that we might learn the undefeatedness of God!

Then we should notice also, at Bethel, that in spite of Jacob's spiritual condition, God has not one word of rebuke for him. We would certainly have had! Yet God made no mention of what had happened. He knew all about Jacob and his deceit and his subtle contriving. Here was this man, determined to reach his goal no matter what means he used to get there, and God knew he was like that. But for that very reason, God did not rebuke him. It would have been no use; he was like that, he could not change, and God did not tell him to. God knew that Jacob was in His hands; and what Jacob could not do, God Himself could.

Twenty-one years later, when Jacob came back to Bethel, he was a different man, and God knew this would be so.

What is not accomplished in ten years will be in twenty. At the end of that time God is still loving. He has not forgotten, and He never approved of Jacob's action. Jacob was foolish, but God had His plans. Time would work them out.

This promise to Jacob was greater and went further than that given to either Abraham or Isaac. "Behold, I am with you and will keep you wherever you go, and will bring you back to this land; for I will not leave you until I have done what I have spoken to you" (28:15). Praise God for this extra promise given to Jacob! It was unconditional. There was no "if you . . . then I. . . ." Whatever Jacob was like by nature, God had a plan; He would have His way. He has a way to His goal for even the most hopeless of us. He cannot be defeated. There is no means of bringing God to a halt halfway there.

From Bethel onward Jacob was in God's hand, and twenty years of discipline brought about the change in him. But here, at the outset of his journey, he as yet did not know the meaning of the promise. This revelation to Jacob in a dream had not changed him one bit. To look at him only draws from us the exclamation: "Lord, Your work is indeed so perfect, but how poor the material You have to work upon!"

From verses 16 and 17 it seems that, on waking, Jacob had forgotten what God had said, and was only afraid because he had slept at the gate of heaven. The promise was secondary. He was afraid of God. And the house of God is indeed a terrifying place to those in whom the flesh has not been dealt with. The house of God has the power of God—God's order, holiness, righteousness—revealed in it. It is justly to be feared if the flesh is still proud and active.

Then Jacob spoke to God. "Then Jacob made a vow,

saying, 'If God will be with me, and keep me in this way that I am going, and give me bread to eat and clothing to put on, so that I come back to my father's house in peace, then the LORD shall be my God. And this stone which I have set up as a pillar shall be God's house'" (20–21). What a contrast this is to God's unqualified words to him. Jacob says, "If . . . if . . . if . . . then." We see here what Jacob's desires were: namely, food and clothing. He had lost sight of God's purpose. But surely here we can already detect God's discipline. For he was young, the beloved of his mother; and now he was alone, knowing nothing of his future. Even in this situation his chastening had begun. He wanted food and clothing, and to return to his home! "And of all that You give me I will surely give a tenth to You" (28:22). That is Jacob! If You give me all this, then I will give You a tenth! He wanted to do business, even with God. Everything for him was on a commercial basis.

Yet this was also Bethel—God's house. Although Jacob could not rise to God's promise, yet from that time, to Jacob He was the God of Bethel. A great impression was made on Jacob there.

Now Jacob comes to Haran, and in Genesis 29:9–11 we read how Rachel was the first one of his relations to meet him. Again we see God's discipline at work, for the first thing he did was to weep. She awoke in him memories of his past, and of the way he had come. Before he left home he had been hard; there had been plenty of ways of keeping himself from tears. It is those who have no way out of their situation who weep. Jacob's course had led him from riches to poverty. Again God had touched and chastened him.

For one whole month Jacob was a guest in his relatives'

home (29:14). After that Laban said to him, "Because you are my relative, should you therefore serve me for nothing? Tell me, what should your wages be?" (v. 15). Yet verse 14 contains no suggestion that Jacob had been serving Laban! His host was announcing a change of status.

The fact is, both Laban and Jacob had commercial minds. The natural man and the worldly man are one in this. On Jacob there were a lot of sharp corners to be rubbed off, and whereas Esau could not rub him, Laban certainly could. There is plenty of friction when two of the same kind meet and live together! First it had been, "my bone and my flesh" (v. 14). Now it is, "You work and I will pay you." It was a polite way of saying, "You can't live here for nothing!"

In his own home Jacob had been the son; all was his. Now Jacob was a servant, a cattleman, and his uncle was a harsh taskmaster. Once more God's chastening hand was at work.

But there was still more to come. Jacob served Laban seven years for the hand of his daughter Rachel, his first love, and then Laban cheated him! He gave him Leah instead. It is always very bitter to have to take your own medicine! So Jacob served another seven years—fourteen years in all for Laban's two daughters. He went out to keep the sheep, and Laban changed his wages ten times. Thus Jacob was put through the fires of discipline, tested and tried, but with the hand of God always upon him. For God had promised to bring Jacob back home.

Laban could scheme and plan as ably as Jacob; indeed, even Jacob had difficulty in getting the better of him. Yet somehow he managed it. He schemed long and carefully to increase his own flock and to enhance his wealth at the expense of his uncle, and in his scheming he makes it quite clear that he has not changed one bit!

Yet Jacob acknowledged the hand of God. Though through all the years he had not mentioned God's name, yet at last, with the birth of Joseph, he bethought himself of home and sought to return (30:25). But now he could not get away! He was in fact compelled to stay on with such a man as Laban for twenty long years.

What God's hand does is right. Circumstances are His appointment for our good. They are calculated to undermine and weaken the specially strong points of our nature. It may not take Him as much as twenty years to do this, or it may take longer. Yet God knows what He is doing. We see this clearly at the end of Jacob's life. Earlier he had inspired little affection in anyone, for everyone had to serve his ends; yet at the last he became gentle and lovable.

"Now for a little while, if need be, you have been grieved by various trials, that the genuineness of your faith, being much more precious than gold that perishes, though it is tested by fire, may be found to praise, honor, and glory at the revelation of Jesus Christ" (1 Peter 1:6–7). There is nothing accidental in the life of the believer. It is all measured out to us. We may not welcome the discipline, but it is designed in the end to make us partakers of His holiness.

14

The Divine Wounding

ISAAC'S LIFE was peaceful, with no strivings. Jacob's way was one long struggle throughout. For Isaac everything went easily; Jacob found even the simplest things presenting difficulties. God is the God of Abraham, Isaac, and Jacob, all three; so we cannot have Isaac without Jacob, nor—praise God!—Jacob without Isaac.

We ourselves are in the position of both. From the Lord's side we are rich, complete in Christ. Yet because of our own natural strength, God's hand has a chastening and formative work to do upon us. We cannot escape the discipline, but equally surely we shall never be without the absolute fullness of divine bestowal. If there is a difference in the discipline it is because some of us have more of Jacob to be dealt with than do others. That is all!

Proverbs 13:15 tells us that "the way of transgressors is hard," that is, tough or rugged. Jacob's way was like that because he was like that. The hard, rugged self in Jacob re-

quired a lot of time for God to deal with it, and many of us
will be of little use unless God has taken significant time to
handle us. Jacob was a usurper and a cheat. God will not let
such a man escape.

Some ask why God spent so much time on Jacob, as
though it were an easy thing to deal with any man! To receive, as Isaac received, is something done in a minute. We
enter into our inheritance as soon as our hearts respond with
a thank-you to what God reveals. But Jacob's difficulty is a
lifelong thing. As long as we live, our natural strength pur-
sues us. It is always being dealt with by God, though there is
a time when this is specially true.

Those who do not know themselves do not know Jacob.
We need to be aware how the flesh always takes care of itself,
cheating others to do so—and being cheated—if we are going to understand this man. For with all God's dealings with
him in Laban's home, Jacob was still largely unchanged.
Cheating, scheming, planning, were yet in his character.

But as we have seen, after twenty years and with the birth
of Joseph, Jacob bethought himself of home (30:25). Then
it was that for the first time in Haran God spoke to him.
"Return to the land of your fathers and to your family, and I
will be with you." And again: "I am the God of Bethel, where
you anointed the pillar and where you made a vow to Me.
Now arise, get out of this land, and return to the land of
your family" (31:3, 13). So Jacob prepared himself to go.

But Laban was not likely to let him go easily. In spite of
everything, God had blessed Laban for Jacob's sake. So Jacob
left secretly, and Laban followed him. But it was God who
had sent Jacob back, and God protected him. At God's time
He sets us free. When the testing has accomplished its pur-

pose, God lets us go, and no man, not even Laban, can keep us.

When Laban eventually caught up with Jacob they made a covenant together. Laban was respectful and he swore by the God of Abraham and of Nahor. Jacob swore, however, by the God of his father Isaac (31:51–53). He bore witness to the fact that God's promise was according to God's choice.

Then Jacob offered a sacrifice (31:54). Laban had none. Something surely had happened to Jacob. When he first went out it was his mother who sent him. Now God sends him home, and he goes. He has learned to recognize God's voice. Discipline had not changed him much, but he had at least advanced into wanting God. In his early years he had wanted only God's purpose, because it fitted in with his desires. He wanted God's will, but not God Himself. Now at last he had some desire for *Him*. He had heard His voice, and now he sacrificed.

"Then Laban departed and returned to his place. So Jacob went on his way, and the angels of God met him. When Jacob saw them, he said, 'This is God's host.' And he called the name of that place Mahanaim" (31:55—32:2). Jacob had left Laban, having been protected from him by God. Now angels met him. God had opened Jacob's eyes to see that just as He had delivered him from Laban, so He would deliver him from everyone else. The name Mahanaim means "two companies." Not you alone, Jacob, one company— but always God's company with you. It was not that the angels had just arrived, but that Jacob's eyes were at last opened to see them. "'Do not fear, for those who are with us are more than those who are with them.' And Elisha prayed, and said, 'LORD, I pray, open his eyes that he may see.' Then the LORD opened the eyes of the young man, and he saw. And behold, the mountain was full of horses and chariots of fire all around Elisha" (2 Kings 6:16–17).

At this point, we may well ask, could all the conditions possibly be more favorable for Jacob? He had God's command, God's promise, God's protection, and now a vision of the angels with him. Surely this was enough to make anyone trust God! But Jacob was still Jacob. God's grace does not alter the flesh. So in the following verses Jacob sends a very lowly, flattering message to his brother Esau. "My lord . . . your servant . . ." he says (32:3–4). He had already forgotten God's call and His grace and His protection. He thought his own specious words could somehow change Esau. That was Jacob still, just the same as he ever was!

But Esau started out to meet him with four hundred men. What did that mean? Good or bad? It struck dismay in Jacob's heart. Clever people have many worries; schemers pile up troubles for themselves. Those who think and contrive, and do not trust and believe, find themselves like Jacob, "greatly afraid" and "distressed" (32:7).

Jacob's one problem, as always, was what to *do*! But, trust him, he still had plans! God had sent him now to Canaan, so he could not flee back to Mesopotamia. Yet he dare not let God look after the results of his obedience. How many of us obey God by the front door and make preparations to retreat by the back! Jacob tried both to obey God and at the same time to escape his brother.

In his fear and distress, we are told that Jacob "divided the people that were with him, and the flocks and herds and camels, into two companies" (32:7). Here we find the same word, "mahanaim," that occurred in verse 2. Jacob had substituted his Mahanaim for God's. There had been one earthly company and one heavenly one, but he divided his earthly company into two! So, perhaps, he would impress his brother, who would scarcely have eyes for the unseen!

Now in verses 9–12 we have Jacob's first real prayer. He has made some progress, though it has not yet reached a high level. In his early years it was all scheming and bargaining, and no prayer. Now it is both scheming and prayer. Yet if we pray, we need not scheme. If we scheme, there is often no meaning in our prayer. But Jacob still did both; on the one hand he trusted God, on the other hand he did the work himself! To trust God completely would be too reckless, for suppose God's words fell empty to the ground! How like us he was! "Of course, I am a Christian; so I must trust God"; but to trust Him fully and completely is taking too great a risk.

So Jacob elaborated his plans (32:13–18). Remember, this man had just prayed! This stratagem, however, was to be his masterpiece. Of course he knew his brother, that he was a hunter—so he truly faced the most dangerous crisis of his life. Never before had he expended so much thought and effort as he put into this. After all, more than his possessions, his very life itself depended on the outcome.

But Jacob was equal to the situation. He who had been through all these years of God's discipline could still summon the wits to produce an answer. In a series of mollifying gestures he would let everything go if necessary to Esau, and so at least save his skin. It was a great scheme, the best he had ever made. Moreover, he believed in his own plans and trusted to them—and yet *he had prayed*! He looked to God—and made the most elaborate preparations.

It was on that night that God met him. There had never

been a night when he was more afraid. On previous occasions it did not so much matter whether he succeeded or not. This time it was a matter of life and death to him. He had used all his wits, all his strength, to meet a most difficult situation, and everything hung on the outcome.

All the others had passed on across the ford. Remaining behind on this side, "Jacob was left alone" (32:24). Here at Peniel God met him face to face. "And a Man wrestled with him until the breaking of day." Now it was that Jacob put forth his utmost strength.

It was not Jacob who wrestled, but God who came and wrestled with him, to bring about his utter surrender. The object of wrestling is to force a man down until he is unable to move, so that he yields to the victor. Yet of God it is said that even here "He did not prevail" (v. 25). Jacob possessed tremendous natural strength. Many of us know all too well what this means. We can still do so well ourselves; we employ all sorts of natural skills for our self-protection. It is as if God were defeated.

Defeat is defeat. When you or I are defeated it means "I cannot," "I yield." Yet being as we are, we have another try. God may overthrow our plans again and again, but we don't admit defeat, we do not give up. We just think we have not planned well enough, and the next time we must do better. "Is anything too hard for the Lord?" the angel had exclaimed to Abraham (18:14). But it is almost as if we say to the Lord, "Is anything too hard for *me*?"!

One day we must acknowledge defeat, confessing that we know nothing at all and can do nothing at all. Jacob had yet to come there, and still thought he knew Esau! For this last step, therefore, something more than discipline was necessary. Discipline brought Jacob as far as Peniel, and it brings us to the place where God can touch us fundamentally. But beware of boasting about God's disciplinary dealings, for until the question of our natural strength is finally settled, this kind of talk can only increase our pride.

Wrestling illustrates God's method of dealing with us. It is finally to weaken us so that we cannot rise. God has His way of doing this with each of us. Jacob was stronger than most, but God conquered. Had he used other means it might have meant a further twenty years. But when Jacob would not yield, God "touched him." With a touch He did what great strength would not do.

The thigh is the strongest part of the body, a fitting type of our point of greatest natural strength. There must come a day when God dislocates that thigh, totally undermining and undoing our strength of nature. Your strong point and mine may be quite different from Jacob's. Ambition, boasting, emotion, self-love—each of us has his own, but for each of us this dislocating work is a definite crisis of experience.

With some of us, as we said, the trouble is a readiness to expose spiritual things. In all our work and life and conduct, the fruits are brought out on the surface and displayed. Exposure is in such a case the nerve center of our natural strength, and God must touch that. Self is dominant there. People's mistakes vary, and many of us have never seen where our nerve center is. But generally all our mistakes spring from one inner principle, and when all symptoms point to one disease, that is our "thigh." May God open our eyes to see the nerve center of our natural strength, for when that is touched, then there will be fruitfulness.

One touch—and Jacob was lamed. He could no longer

wrestle; he was powerless. Dawn came, and he said to God, "I will not let You go." But when any member, even a finger, is dislocated, the whole body is put out of action. Speaking physically, if God had wanted to go He could perfectly well have gone off and left Jacob there. Jacob could not possibly have held Him.

But now that Jacob was truly weak the Wrestler *could* not leave him. For Jacob depended on Him. It is when our thigh has been touched that we can hold God the closest. We are strongest when we are weakest (2 Corinthians 12:10). From man's standpoint this looks impossible, but it is divine fact. It is small faith that accomplishes great things. "I cannot hold You, but I can plead with You! I can scarcely even pray, yet I can plead. I have no faith, yet I believe!"

With an abundance of natural strength we are useless to God. With no strength at all, we can hold onto Him. God's response to Jacob was amazing. "Your name shall no longer be called Jacob, but Israel; for you have struggled with God and with men, and have prevailed" (32:28). Ten years experience looked like defeat for Jacob, but God said he had prevailed. This is what happens when we surrender, beaten, at God's feet.

"Then Jacob asked, saying, 'Tell me Your name, I pray.' And He said, 'Why is it that you ask about My name?' And He blessed him there." Jacob wanted to know who had done this, but he was not told. Jacob did not know who the Wrestler was when He came, and he knew no more when He went. He just knew that his own name had been changed—and that he limped! This is the only time in Scripture when God declined to reveal His name to a servant of His.

Those touched by God do not know what has happened.

When it really takes place, we don't know what it is. That is why it is so difficult to define, for God does not want us to wait for an experience. If we do, we shall not get it. God wants our eye fixed on *Him*, not on experiences. Jacob only knew that somehow God had met him, and that now he was crippled. The *limp* is the evidence, not merely the witness of one's lips. We are to look to God to do the work in His own way and time. The result will be evident in us, and there will be no need to talk about it.

15

The Face of God

THERE is one very striking
peculiarity about the history
of Jacob; namely, that God never preached to him, He only
gave him promises.

Jacob was a man who stopped at nothing to accomplish
his ends. What would we do with such a man? Surely we
would at least exhort him a little, maybe preach to him about
his failings. Yet from beginning to end, God never once gave
him one such word of rebuke or exhortation. Both Pharaoh
and Abimelech reproved Abraham; Abimelech again rebuked
Isaac—yet nothing like this happened to Jacob. But God
worked. Without stopping to exhort or to explain, God dis-
ciplined him.

And God *encouraged* Jacob. The first time, at Bethel, God
promised, "Behold, I am with you." And He was! He led
him. One's natural strength cannot be changed by doctrine;
we can be delivered from it only by God's chastening, step
by step, until it is broken. And if God did not stay with us in

this we would certainly never go through with it. Jacob never longed to make progress; he never wanted to be spiritual or to follow the example of Abraham and Isaac. God Himself sought him out and stayed with him and dealt with him over those long years, until at last at Peniel, when Jacob had produced his masterpiece of self-expression, God brought him to his knees and he yielded the mastery. God did every bit of it! We can well afford to trust the discipline of the Spirit.

We have God's words aplenty, but we forget His discipline. We sometimes think that to hear sound doctrine is the sole means of grace; but if we are His, the Spirit disciplines us all the time just as He did Jacob. He prepares for us a host of different circumstances, just with this one object. Everything in our lives is directed by Him to this end, to bring us to the place of Israel. God is an acting God. He will never let us go. Everything the believer meets is measured to him by God. The chastening we experience is for our profit.

If we are His, then, however bad material we are, God follows us. He is more tenacious than we are. We would need to be greater than God before we could prevent Him from doing His work. While we are only men, natural men, God will have His way. While Jacob is there, however bad, God will pursue His goal of an Israel. Trust His tenaciousness, count on His invincibility. Look to Him, and in His time and His way, He will finish the work.

There is a further ground of encouragement. We do not have to know what work is needed, or what is going on, in order that God may do the work He has set Himself to do. True, the most pitiable people are those who are wrong and do not know it, for darkness is added to their wrong. But we may be the most pitiable people and still God will take us in hand. Jacob, as we saw, was up against the most difficult situation in his life. His wives, his children, his possessions, himself—all the things which were most precious to him were in danger. Other people's things had never mattered to him; now, however, it was his own interests that were at stake, so he made the most detailed and careful plan.

Jacob did not know that he was exposing the nerve center of his strength. Esau had been brought onto the scene again by God so that the strength of nature might be fully discovered and exposed. It is God who leads us to it, bringing about circumstances in which we discover ourselves.

The whole meaning of Peniel is here. Our natural life has a life principle which ordinarily we do not recognize. God may take pains to point it out to us, but we do not see it at all until we come to a place like Jacob's Mahanaim, when God brings into jeopardy the thing we have been most proud of. That *pride* is the thing God hates. The revelation of that natural strength *kills* what it reveals. Is there something we secretly boast of? Something we are very careful of because it represents our greatest achievement, the best feature of ourselves? When God touches that, we are too ashamed to live. God's touch brings not only weakness but shame.

Peniel is "the face of God." "I have seen God face to face," said Jacob, "and my life is preserved" (32:30). God uses light to expose to us the true situation, and that is what brings us down to the ground. The light exposes what is the true spring and motive of our life. God in mercy must bring us there, where we see that all we have boasted of and gloried in is shame.

Remember, God is dealing with what we really are by nature, and at Peniel He begins His work. For there, in the light of God, we must be as we are—we cannot pretend. Pretense is not Christianity! We may very much want to be different, but what we are by nature, we are. Nothing hinders God more than our pretending it is otherwise. The more "humble" some people are, the more one wishes they would show a little pride, because that would give God a chance to get on with the work. For it is never our pretense but only God's *touch* that brings about the transformation. If the work is to be done by me, it will get me nowhere. From being "natural" I shall merely become unnatural. But if the work is God's work, the change wrought by Him has a definite purpose and direction. From Jacob He changes us to Israel.

Many of us do not know what has happened at Peniel until later on. We don't know quite how or when it happened, but things are inconvenient; it hurts to run! It is the peculiarity of the touch of God that we cannot now do the things we used to like doing. In speech, for example, we used to be confident, but now we are hesitant and uncomfortable. With Paul we say, "I was with you in weakness, in fear, and in much trembling. And my speech and my preaching were not with persuasive words of human wisdom, but in demonstration of the Spirit and of power" (1 Corinthians 2:3–4). We go and we serve God, and we speak because God wants the task done and not because, as once we did, we find enjoyment or gratification or comfort in doing it. We shall do the work, but fundamentally it will be God who does it and not us.

Peniel is God's new start; it is not perfection. There for the first time Jacob was named "Israel"; yet after that he was

still called Jacob very often. There was much that lacked in
him, which may be the reason why God did not tell him His
own name there. Peniel is a turning point. Abraham's road
had led to Shechem and on from there to Bethel and Hebron.
These, as we have seen, were places characteristic of the land.
It was after Peniel that God led Jacob over Abraham's road.

Yet even after Peniel, Jacob went on with his plans. If we
know ourselves, we shall not blame him. To change in a night
is not an earthly thing; it requires the work of heaven. But
the fact is that after Peniel Jacob's strength had gone. We
easily call a halt to Jacob, but we do not so easily stop ourselves. Let us not interpret the Bible by theory but see it in
the light of experience. Yes, Jacob went right on pursuing
the course he had been following before God met him.

When he met Esau, he discovered that he had wasted his
time! "Esau ran to meet him, and embraced him, and fell on
his neck and kissed him" (33:4). All the crafty and calculat-
ing preparation had been to no purpose. Esau was ready to
be reconciled.

It is good to notice the conversation that follows. "But
Esau said, 'I have enough, my brother; keep what you have
for yourself.' And Jacob said, 'No, please, if I have now found
grace in your sight, then receive my present from my hand,
inasmuch as I have seen your face as though I had seen the
face of God, and you were pleased with me'" (33:9–10).
Jacob's form of address to his brother may seem unduly flattering, but we should not regard this as simply a bit more of
Jacob's scheming, however much there may have been of
pretense in his humility. There was fact here also. "I have
seen your face as though I had seen the face of God." Those
we have wronged will always represent God to us. When we

meet them, we meet God; and we are judged, unless the thing is settled. How deep were the lessons God was teaching Jacob through this encounter with Esau!

"So Esau returned that day on his way to Seir. And Jacob journeyed to Succoth, and built himself a house, and made booths for his livestock. Therefore the name of the place is called Succoth. Then Jacob came safely to the city of Shechem, which is in the land of Canaan, when he came from Padan Aram; and he pitched his tent before the city. And he bought the parcel of land, where he had pitched his tent, from the children of Hamor, Shechem's father, for one hundred pieces of money. Then he erected an altar there, and called it El Elohe Israel" (33:16–20). Jacob did now what neither Abraham nor Isaac had done: he built a house and he bought land. He left his tent! But he also built an altar to God, the God of Israel. He was not yet perfect—had not yet reached Bethel—and whereas God had set his fathers in tents, he had built a house. Yes, he had advanced. But there was trouble in Shechem. God would not leave him at peace, but let him meet very bad trouble (chapter 34) which would never have occurred had he not settled in Shechem. His very name became offensive to the inhabitants, and his whole household was put in jeopardy.

Then at last Jacob was sent by God to Bethel. "Then God said to Jacob, 'Arise, go up to Bethel and dwell there; and make an altar there to God, who appeared to you when you fled from the face of Esau your brother'" (35:1). There at Bethel God completed His work, for nothing could touch Jacob's heart like Bethel. It was the place where his long experience had begun.

Bethel is God's house, the place where divine power is

manifested through the Body of Christ. It is a place into which we dare not bring anything that is not of God. "Put away the foreign gods that are among you, purify yourselves, and change your garments. Then let us arise and go up to Bethel; and I will make an altar there to God, who answered me in the day of my distress and has been with me in the way which I have gone" (35:2–3).

As we saw in the life of Abraham, Shechem represents strength—the strength of Christ with us, enabling us to deal with everything. That strength is ours to prepare us for entering into God's house; for when we arrive there, holiness will not be merely personal but corporate. In the Body of Christ, all is of God.

"And he built an altar there and called the place El Bethel," that is, the God of Bethel. At Shechem He was the God of Israel; now He is the God of Bethel. Jacob had moved on from individualism to relatedness in the Body. God wanted a house, a people, for a vessel. He cannot fulfill His purpose without a corporate witness. In the Church God is the God of Bethel, not just *my* God.

"Then God appeared to Jacob again, when he came from Padan Aram, and blessed him. And God said to him, 'Your name is Jacob; your name shall not be called Jacob anymore, but Israel shall be your name.' So He called his name Israel" (35:9–10). God appeared, and not in a dream this time. He came at Bethel to confirm and complete what Peniel had begun. Jacob was no longer the rascal, the usurper—he was God's prince. That which begins when we see the light of God is completed in the house of God.

At Bethel God addressed Jacob with the words, "I am God Almighty." It was the same address that He had used to

Abraham. "I am no longer concerned merely to expose your helplessness, I am here to affirm My might." God can speak like this to Jacob because now He has a vessel according to His heart.

Again Jacob set up a pillar at Bethel (v. 14) and this time he did something he did not do before: he poured over it a drink offering, typifying joy. The first time he came to this place it was "a dreadful place" and he only feared. Now he rejoiced. And now the way was opened for him to go forward to Hebron.

16

The Peaceable Fruit

IT IS now time to glance over the latter part of Jacob's history and see the evidences of the fruitfulness in him of all this inward discipline by the Spirit of God. Already, when Jacob met Esau, he was different. We find him uncertain, hesitant, not quite knowing what to do, though clearly he still has in him a good deal of his old nature. Genesis 33:4 tells us that he wept. Jacob did not weep easily. People with plenty of plans do not; but Peniel had already weakened him.

At Peniel Jacob's name was changed; and as we have just seen, the same change was repeated at Bethel. Between the two there was a period of weakness and confusion, and this often happens after God has once touched us. We have to learn to walk gently and very carefully with God, and the lesson is not easy. Peniel therefore represents weakness, whereas Bethel stands for cleanness and purity with no mixture at all. Moving from Peniel to Bethel we pass through a strange town, Shechem. We are weakened, and we do not know quite where we are, nor whether if we move again we shall go wrong once more. But praise God, His work has begun, and the foundation has been laid. There is no way now of not being a cripple!

We shall always be learning, but at some point we will each learn that fundamental lesson—after which nothing can be the same again. From that point there begins a knowledge of God beyond anything we have ever dreamed. With it we enter upon a new experience of the life of the Body, drawing us together with all His own. This is a setting in which the fruit of the Holy Spirit's inward working readily manifests itself. Thus from Bethel we are told that "Jacob came to his father Isaac at Mamre, or Kirjath Arba (that is, Hebron), where Abraham and Isaac had dwelt" (35:27). Hebron represents fellowship, mutuality, the place where nothing can be done individually and in isolation. Until the flesh has been dealt with we do not value fellowship. We find it easy and natural to go it alone. But now we find the significance of being "together."

Fellowship means among other things that we are ready to receive of Christ from others. Other believers minister Christ to me, and I am ready to receive. This may be an important lesson, for some are born teachers who are always preaching to others and have no use at all for receiving from anyone else. If I am like that, I surely need to meet my Peniel. Only then can I come to Bethel and Hebron. But when we have come there, we know in our hearts that we cannot live without others—that alone by ourselves we have no place, no ground to stand upon. The Body is a divine fact. Just as no member of our body can live without all the rest, just as the eye cannot say to the hand, "I have no need of you," or again the head to the feet, "I have no need of you," so is the Body of Christ a sphere of interdependence. How significant, then, when Jacob at length reached Hebron and was restored to the fellowship of his home!

This is not to say that Jacob no longer needed God's discipline after Peniel. He did, and he got it. At Shechem he was put in fear of his life (34:30). At Bethel Rebekah's nurse Deborah died (35:8). On the way to Bethlehem his beloved Rachel herself was taken from him (35:19). At Eder Jacob had more trouble with his sons, this time with Reuben (35:21–22). He reached Hebron to find his mother already dead, and here at length Isaac himself ended his days (35:29). God was disciplining Jacob, working in him a new character, changing him into a different person.

From Genesis 37 onward is Jacob's brightest period. During these remaining thirty years he is full of grace. We need not consider his last days as days of decline; they were certainly not that, and compare quite favorably with those of Peter and Paul and John. In the Old Testament it is Solomon whose last days are days of declension, but these should not be taken as the experience of others. David's end was better even than his beginning, for he was planning and preparing for the building of the Temple. In the same way, Jacob in his last days became gracious and lovable. Comparing his end with that of Abraham and Isaac we cannot fail to see that his is the best. They faded away, as it were, whereas Jacob bore fruit. God revealed Himself in this unpromising man.

From Genesis 37—that is, from the time Joseph was seventeen—Jacob retires into the background. Before that he had always been on the go, always active, as though he had an internal combustion engine driving him! He always had some project on hand, and always seemed to have reserves of strength to carry it out. From the day of his birth you could not stop him doing and talking; you could not arrest his perpetual busyness.

But when he reached Hebron, he retired. Sometimes he came forward to speak or to act, but it was just sometimes. He had nothing any longer driving him to this incessant doing. Seeing what Jacob was—for remember, he was himself quite unable to let off the pressure—this was a most remarkable thing. But Jacob now is a very lovely character. He is quietly, blessedly fruitful.

Isaac is a type of Christ; but Jacob is a type of the natural man. So Jacob must stop his incessant driving. The Isaac side, the spiritual strength, must go on, but the natural strength must come to a halt. Now Jacob is in the background; there is no other place suitable for him. The movement of the flesh has to cease when God has dealt with it.

Jacob, the cheat, the schemer, lived for himself and cared nothing about others. There was no love expressed in him. But from the time Deborah died, he experienced all sorts of family sorrows and troubles. All those he had loved died. At Hebron he was left with nothing. Even his own eldest son had wronged him. Joseph was the only one left.

But Jacob had begun to be loving. He had ripened and mellowed. He was anxious about his sons, afraid of trouble for them, concerned for their welfare. He wanted to know how they fared, and so he sent Joseph to inquire.

Then Joseph also disappeared, and Jacob had every reason to think he was dead. "It is my son's tunic," he said, "a wild beast has devoured him. Without doubt Joseph is torn to pieces" (37:33). Gradually everything he had loved had gone from him, and now this last link with Rachel was broken. "And all his sons and all his daughters arose to comfort him; but he refused to be comforted, and he said, 'For I shall go down into the grave to my son in mourning.' Thus his father wept for him" (37:35). No other verse in Jacob's history is so poignant as this one.

Thirteen years passed by. Joseph had already reached the place of power in Egypt. Again Jacob met with trouble. This time it was famine, and all his wealth was in cattle! So now his material wealth drained away.

There was just one loved possession left, "the youngest" (42:13) who had grown up to take the place of Joseph and who remained with his father. Only little Benjamin was left to Jacob. He was more precious than all the others, but even he was not like Joseph who was lost. When it came to the second time that his sons must go to Egypt to buy food, Simeon was already held in prison there as a hostage, and they could not go again without taking Benjamin with them. Can we not read the pathos in Jacob's words: "You have bereaved me: Joseph is no more, Simeon is no more, and you want to take Benjamin. All these things are against me"? (42:36). Here was a man who had lived under the discipline of God's hand, changed now into a gentle, deeply feeling parent.

But the time came when Benjamin, his last treasure, had to go. And it is here, in Genesis 43, that Jacob comes into his name Israel. "And their father Israel said to them, 'If it must be so, then do this: Take some of the best fruits of the land in your vessels and carry down a present for the man— a little balm and a little honey, spices and myrrh, pistachio nuts and almonds. Take double money in your hand, and take back in your hand the money that was returned in the mouth of your sacks; perhaps it was an oversight. Take your brother also, and arise, go back to the man'" (43:11–13). Here was a man, weak and uncertain in himself, who could listen to the counsel of his sons. In these proposals he displays, surely, not the stratagems of the past, but the courtesy and kindness of maturity and experience. "And may God Almighty give you mercy before the man, that he may release your other brother and Benjamin." Now, for the first time, Jacob speaks like this, using the name he learned at Bethel. How different he is! How God has stripped him of his confidence. "If I am bereaved, I am bereaved!" he cries, but yet he hopes that God will have mercy. Knowing ourselves, and looking at Jacob with that inward knowledge, we realize what God has done. Jacob has not yet reached his highest peak, the seventeen years in Egypt. Here there is still discipline, but there is evident fruitfulness.

His sons returned at length with news of Joseph. "Joseph is still alive, and he is governor over all the land of Egypt" (45:26). Again he is Israel. Had it been twenty years earlier, Jacob would have cursed his sons for deceiving him all this time. But not now—now he is mature; now his meekness shines forth. "Then Israel said, 'It is enough. Joseph my son is still alive. I will go and see him before I die.'" He had learned deep lessons.

But though his father-heart longed to go to Joseph, yet he feared (46:1). Abraham had gone into Egypt and had sinned. Isaac had been on his way thither and had been forbidden to go. Could he, even for Joseph's sake, go down into Egypt now? His natural love for his son must not be allowed to interfere with God's purpose.

So he stopped halfway—and here for the first time Jacob really shines. He came to Beersheba, and offered sacrifices to the God of his father Isaac. He laid his all on the altar. "To go, or not to go? The decision is Yours, for I am Yours." This was his attitude to God.

And God answered him. "I am God, the God of your father; do not fear to go down to Egypt, for I will make of you a great nation there. I will go down with you to Egypt, and I will also surely bring you up again; and Joseph will put his hand on your eyes" (46:3–4). That "fear not" shows us Jacob's fear; thank God for it! It shows us too the reality of God's work upon him; for in this hesitation he proves that he had gone further than either Abraham or Isaac. God did not have to stop him at Beersheba. Jacob himself stopped, and took his stand upon the basis of the altar. In these verses we see a different man entirely. Spiritual principles are ruling him now; he cannot just please himself.

So they came at last to Egypt. "Then Joseph brought in his father Jacob and set him before Pharaoh; and Jacob blessed Pharaoh. Pharaoh said to Jacob, 'How old are you?' And Jacob said to Pharaoh, 'The days of the years of my pilgrimage are one hundred and thirty years; few and evil have been the days of the years of my life, and they have not attained to the days of the years of the life of my fathers in the days of their pilgrimage.' So Jacob blessed Pharaoh, and went out from before Pharaoh" (47:7–10).

What a picture this is! Where can we find a better? Who is this Jacob after all? Even Joseph was less than Pharaoh in the kingdom, and Jacob himself was in fact no more than a refugee! He was dependent upon Pharaoh for his very survival.

Pharaoh was his benefactor. Years ago Jacob had called Esau "lord." But now? Now he blessed *Pharaoh*. "Now beyond all contradiction the lesser is blessed by the greater" (Hebrews 7:7), and Jacob knew he was the greater. For Jacob was now living in a different world, a world where he stood before God. Pharaoh king of Egypt was the greatest monarch in the earth at that time. No nation in the world was stronger than Egypt, so we would hardly blame Jacob if he had taken a servile attitude before him. But all the old false humility had gone, and he stood on his new ground and blessed Pharaoh. In just such a way Paul dared to express his wishes for the spiritual good of king Agrippa (Acts 26:29): "I would to God that not only you, but also all who hear me today, might become . . . such as I am, except for these chains." My fetters apart, my happiness is greater than yours—yes, even yours O king!

"Few and bitter have been the days of my pilgrimage." Jacob felt things. He honestly felt now that his life had not approached that of his fathers. Again he blessed Pharaoh, and then quietly went out from his presence. How likable this old man had become! It would have been very easy for him now to have secured some glory for himself out of Joseph's position. But he did not seek this. He remained in the background, and that is where we must look for him now, for we cannot find him in the foreground. The Jacob of long ago would have grasped at this chance of prominence and fame, and there is no telling what he might have made out of it. But now he is no longer Jacob; he is Israel. His very unobtrusiveness is the mark of God's great work in him, and is his greatest value to God.

There remain seventeen years of his life, in which nothing much seems to happen, but he goes on advancing and shining ever more brightly. May God give to every one of us such an end.

"When the time drew near that Israel must die, he called his son Joseph and said to him, 'Now if I have found favor in your sight, please put your hand under my thigh, and deal kindly and truly with me. Please do not bury me in Egypt, but let me lie with my fathers; you shall carry me out of Egypt and bury me in their burial place'" (47:29–30). This is very notable indeed. There is no word from Jacob about how he should live in Egypt; only of how he should be buried! His death and burial were connected with the promise, the land, the covenant, and the kingdom. He cared nothing about the things he saw around him; only about these that lay in the unseen. The old Jacob had been hard and severe. He had rebuked even Joseph for his dreams (37:10). Now, thirty years later, he says to his own son, "Please, if now I have found favor in your sight. . . ." There was not even a command here, but an altogether new mellowness. "And Joseph said, 'I will do as you have said.' Then he said, 'Swear to me.' And he swore to him. So Israel bowed himself on the head of the bed." In the New Testament it states that he "worshiped, leaning upon the top of his staff" (Hebrews 11:21). He was still a cripple, and he was still a pilgrim.

We have now an old man's memories, but it is very striking to note what in fact Jacob remembered. "God Almighty appeared to me at Luz in the land of Canaan and blessed me" (48:3). "But as for me, when I came from Padan, Rachel died beside me in the land of Canaan on the way, when there was but a little distance to go to Ephrath; and I buried her there on the way to Ephrath (that is, Bethlehem)" (48:7). He remembers his bond with God Almighty; and he remembers his sorrows, that one he so greatly loved should have died before reaching their destination: *this* was Jacob now, toward God, and toward men.

There follows the blessing of Joseph's sons. "Israel stretched out his right hand and laid it on Ephraim's head, who was the younger, and his left hand on Manasseh's head, guiding his hands wittingly, for Manasseh was the firstborn." When Joseph protested and, thinking his father mistaken, tried to remove his hand from Ephraim's head to Manasseh's, Jacob refused to be corrected. "I know, my son, I know," he assured him. Here once again we see him going beyond his father Isaac. What Isaac did in blessing the younger son he did in ignorance, not knowing what he was doing; but here Jacob certainly knew what he was at. Both men were blind, but Isaac was blind inwardly. Jacob certainly was not; his spiritual insight overcame the weakness of his body. "His younger brother shall be greater than he, and his descendants shall become a multitude of nations."

We come at last to the long prophecy concerning the sons of Jacob in Genesis 49. For Jacob was a prophet who had acquired a true insight into God's purposes. In this he was more than either Abraham or Isaac. But what a price he paid for this prophecy! For he was compelled to refer to his children's past, and how he must have seen himself in them! This gave him a sympathy, an understanding, altogether different from the old Jacob. At Shechem there had been a bitterness in his words to Simeon and Levi: "You have troubled me by making me obnoxious among the inhabitants of the land, among the Canaanites and the Perizzites; and since I am few in number, they will gather themselves together against me and kill me. I shall be destroyed, my household and I" (34:30). Now in verses 5–7 of chapter 49 this personal vindictiveness has gone, and it is the sin which concerns him. "Let not my soul enter their council; let not my honor be united to their assembly." His motives had been purified through entering into God's suffering over sin. And look too at his expression of trust, after he had described the future rebellion of Dan: "I have waited for your salvation, O LORD!" (49:18).

At his beginning Jacob had been an utterly hopeless case. But Scripture tells us his story from his birthright through to his death, and to our amazement we find that unpromising man transformed into God's Israel. By the end of Jacob's life the kingdom was already there in the person of this prince with God. If God could make such a vessel out of Jacob, surely He has a plan for us.

In Galatians 6:16 Paul uses the expression "the Israel of God" for the whole of God's people, showing that Israel was herself a type of the Church. "The God of Abraham, Isaac, and Jacob, the God of our fathers, glorified His Servant Jesus," proclaimed Peter, and went on to declare what miracles of divine grace should be accomplished through His name. Yes, God wants His people, all of us, to know Him as the God of Abraham and Isaac and Jacob, all three. He longs to see us motivated by a Father's initiatives, wealthy with the Son's riches, and really transformed by the patient nurture of the Spirit. For through us He has a work to complete, a great purpose for mankind to bring to fulfillment.

PUBLICATIONS

Fort Washington, PA 19034

This book is published by CLC Publications, an outreach of CLC Ministries International. The purpose of CLC is to make evangelical Christian literature available to all nations so that people may come to faith and maturity in the Lord Jesus Christ. We hope this book has been life changing and has enriched your walk with God through the work of the Holy Spirit. If you would like to know more about CLC, we invite you to visit our website:

www.clcusa.org

To know more about the remarkable story of the founding of CLC International we encourage you to read

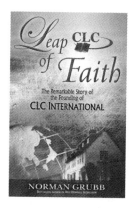

LEAP OF FAITH

Norman Grubb

Paperback
Size 5¹/₄ x 8, Pages 249
ISBN: 978-0-87508-650-7 - $11.99
ISBN (*e-book*): 978-1-61958-055-8 - $9.99

"STIRRING...ORIGINAL...PROVOCATIVE"

WATCHMAN NEE

*L*OVE
NOT
THE
*W*ORLD

A PROPHETIC CALL
TO HOLY LIVING

LOVE NOT THE WORLD

Danger! You're touching the world!

In this hard-hitting and controversial book, Watchman Nee states that there is a Satanic power behind every worldly thing and that the natural tendency of every worldly system such as politics, education, literature, science, art and music is to move away from God and toward Satan.

*How can the Christian live and work in these
systems but not be "of the world"?*

Trade Paper ISBN 0-87508-787-6

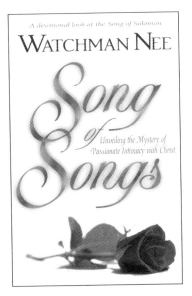

SONG OF SONGS

Watchman Nee believes it is possible to discover within the *Song of Solomon* all the principles needed to develop the spiritual life. In this devotional commentary, he explores the love relationship between the individual believer and the Lord. His insights are for all who long to intensify their love and by so doing find overwhelming joy and complete satisfaction.

Trade Paper ISBN 0-87508-851-1

DAILY DEVOTIONAL MEDITATIONS
FROM THE MINISTRY OF

WATCHMAN NEE

A TABLE
IN THE
WILDERNESS

A TABLE IN THE WILDERNESS

Rich daily devotional thoughts from Watchman Nee

When God spreads for us a **table in the wilderness**, when five loaves provide food for five thousand and leave twelve baskets of fragments, **that is blessing**!

Blessing is fruit all out of relation to what we are. It comes when God works completely beyond our understanding, for His name's sake.

Wonder and gratitude have a high place in these meditations, which are drawn from the author's widely varied ministry in China and beyond. They will draw you again to a fresh response to God's superlative grace in the gift to us of His Son.

Trade Paper ISBN 0-87508-699-3

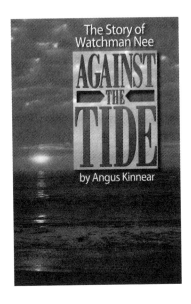

AGAINST THE TIDE

The engrossing, moving biography of one of China's better-known Christians, the dedicated evangelist and gifted Bible teacher Watchman Nee.

Trade Paper ISBN 0-87508-705-1

SIT, WALK, STAND

. . . is an inspiring look at Ephesians which opens our eyes to the central issues of our faith. It describes the process of Christian living and maturity in three words:

SIT — Our posirion in Christ

WALK — Our life in the world

STAND — Our attitude toward the Enemy

These three key words clearly show us the way to victory in this life—and for eternity.

Includes a new Study Guide. An invaluable tool for the growing disciple.

Trade paper   ISBN 978-0-87508-973-7

THE NORMAL CHRISTIAN LIFE

. . . is Watchman Nee's great Christian classic unfolding the central theme of "Christ our Life." Nee reveals the secret of spiritual strength and vitality that should be the normal experience of every Christian.

Trade paper   ISBN   978-0-87508-990-4

THE NORMAL CHRISTIAN LIFE STUDY GUIDE

Gives a brief summary of each chapter of the book and then gives questions designed to provoke thought and possible discussion.

Mass Market   ISBN   0-87508-418-4

Other Titles by Watchman Nee

Aids to Revelation
Assembling Together
Back to the Cross
A Balanced Christian Life
The Body of Christ: A Reality
Christ, the Sum of All Things
Do All to the Glory of God
The Finest of the Wheat, Vol. 1
The Finest of the Wheat, Vol. 2
From Faith to Faith
From Glory to Glory
Full of Grace and Truth, Vol. 1
Full of Grace and Truth, Vol. 2
Gleanings in the Fields of Boaz
The Glory of His Life
God's Plan and the Overcomers
The Good Confession
Gospel Dialogue
Grace for Grace
Interpreting Matthew
The King and the Kingdom of Heaven
The Latent Power of the Soul
Let Us Pray
The Life that Wins

The Lord My Portion
Love One Another
The Messenger of the Cross
The Mystery of Creation
Not I, But Christ
Practical Issues of This Life
The Prayer Ministry of the Church
The Release of the Spirit
    (includes study guide)
Revive Thy Work
The Salvation of the Soul
The Spirit of the Gospel
The Spirit of Judgment
The Spirit of Wisdom and Revelation
Spiritual Authority
Spiritual Knowledge
The Spiritual Man
Spiritual Reality or Obsession
Take Heed
The Testimony of God
What Shall This Man Do?
Whom Shall I Send?
Ye Search the Scriptures